Successful Photography for Writers

SUCCESSFUL PHOTOGRAPHY FOR WRITERS

David Davenport

ROBERT HALE · LONDON

First published in Great Britain 2002

ISBN 0 7090 7130 2

Robert Hale Limited
Clerkenwell House
Clerkenwell Green
London EC1R 0HT

A catalogue record for this book is available from the British Library

2 4 6 8 10 9 7 5 3 1

Typeset in 10.5/15 pt Century Schoolbook
by Derek Doyle & Associates, Liverpool
Printed in Great Britain by
St Edmundsbury Press Limited, Bury St Edmunds
Bound by Woolnough Bookbinding Limited

Contents

Illustrations

Between pages 64 and 65

Between pages 112 and 113

Introduction

Photographs are a welcome bonus when they arrive with a manuscript on an editor's desk. The aim of this book is to encourage writers seeking publication to illustrate their articles with their own photographs. Modern cameras make it easier to take technically good photographs, and, provided you follow the suggested guidelines and produce consistent results, you can achieve publishable images. The effective combination of words plus pictures will considerably increase the chances of getting your articles published.

Even if you are planning a non-fiction book, the recommendations and ideas in this book should help you achieve better images, enabling you to illustrate the manuscript with your own pictures. It will guide you towards a standard of photography that will greatly enhance the chances of your project being accepted.

Writers of fiction, who may use a camera as a pictorial notebook and wish to polish their photographic skills, will also benefit from the numerous tips and advice. Whenever research takes you to a location, your camera can record information about the environment, the people and the way of life. Your photographs will become a valuable source of reference which can help to bring authenticity to your writing.

Photography should not be regarded as an optional extra, but as a valuable extension of your writing. Whether you are photographing a lengthy inscription on a plaque to ensure accuracy or trying to capture the mood of a place, I hope that the concise advice and guidance I provide will help you to develop your skills of seeing and capturing pictures to accompany your words.

1
Words Plus Pictures

Increase Your Chances of Getting Published

Today's publications use illustrations more extensively than ever before. The prominence of pictures, together with innovative design, combine to attract readers to the printed page. That is why a set of pin-sharp, carefully composed photographs submitted with your manuscript will boost your chances of getting your article accepted for publication.

Some writers of illustrated work submit their manuscripts and rely on the editorial office to find appropriate illustrations. Others obtain pictures from press offices or publicity departments whenever possible. And there are also those who enjoy taking the photographs themselves. But there is a fourth category: writers who own a camera and would like to be involved with photography but do not have the self-confidence to take pictures for publication. And of course, there was a time when we took a film to the processors and just hoped that some pictures would 'come out'. But this uncertainty has now been overcome by automatic cameras, improved film emulsions and better processing. Technology now enables photographers to give their undivided attention to the subject instead of being preoccupied with camera settings and adjustments.

A Words-and-Pictures Package

Even if your camera is not equipped with the do-almost-everything features which the latest models offer, be assured that you can learn to acquire an eye for a picture. Provided you follow some basic advice to guide you around the pitfalls that await the unwary, it is possible to take photographs that are quite acceptable for publication. As your confidence and skills increase you will be able to set your sights on creating a words-and-pictures package.

Magazines have several options for obtaining photographs. Some favour picture libraries and agencies, others use their own picture files or commission a photographer. But when editors receive articles accompanied by publishable photographs, it means they have images on their desk available for instant use, and they do not have to spend time finding illustrations elsewhere.

Moreover, if a publisher has to cut costs by reducing editorial staffing levels, this can result in less time being available to source pictures. So an article complete with photographs is going to be even more welcome – provided the package is of a publishable standard and is presented in a professional manner.

The Importance of Market Study

Magazines

Never look upon photographs as an alternative to text, but as an intrinsic part of your feature. Just as you would tailor your writing to the style of a specific journal, plan your pictures with a similar approach. It is essential to carry out a market study by examining previous issues of the magazines in which you hope to be published. In addition to casting an eye over the printed word, analyse the photography as well.

Check the average number of photographs used for each article and the page area they occupy. Make a note of the average size of the pictures, and the type of subjects which are 'blown up', perhaps to page width. Observe whether the pictures are mainly in colour or black and white.

Evaluate each illustration for its qualities as a photograph and then check whether it complements the text. Are any photographs included primarily for impact, and do they reinforce the theme? How prominent are people? Note, too, whether the majority of the pictures are printed in portrait (vertical) or landscape (horizontal) format. If, for example, a magazine seems to prefer a portrait format for most illustrations prepare your submission accordingly.

Magazines differ in content, style and layout. Even those which cater for identical interests vary in approach and presentation. Pictures that look right for one publication may be inappropriate for another. Whatever subject group you are assessing, it is worth trying to identify subtle as well as obvious differences.

By carefully appraising illustrated features overall, and each picture's association with the subject, you will become more adept at recognizing the strengths of photographs which successfully blend with and support the text. Analysing published work will reveal the pictorial content required by particular magazines and give you an idea of the standard required.

Do not skimp on studying the market. Thorough research will save wasted effort when you come to submit your photographs. Consistently aiming at one area of the market can be a successful route to recognition as a writer-photographer, but remember to update your research data regularly.

Get to know the magazines you are targeting by acquiring information from more than one or two copies. Scrutinize at least four consecutive issues of each magazine. These will form the basis of reference material which you can consult whenever research is necessary. Note, too, that from time to time magazines make changes to their format to keep pace with public taste, so market study should be an ongoing exercise.

Set up a file card for each magazine, listing the frequency of publication and telephone and fax details. Ensure that you note the names of the editorial team: editor, assistant editor, features editor, picture editor, etc. When preparing a submission for a magazine based on information collated some months previously, always check that the details are unchanged. Phone the editorial office and confirm whether the person to whom you are writing is still working in the same capacity.

Local Newspapers

Much of the advice on evaluating magazines also applies to newspapers, especially for the writer-photographer seeking to break into one of the local newspapers. Once the editorial staff get to know you as a reliable contributor, there is always a chance that commissions could follow.

When writing for newspapers, remember that when sub-editors reduce the length of text, they tend to cut from the end of the article, so try to ensure that your photographs do not relate only to the closing paragraphs.

Provided your pictures are clear, sharp and carefully composed, the quality of the work should increase the chances of your article being published, but there is always the possibility that a newspaper editor will use staff-produced photographs to illustrate your article.

Letter of Enquiry

Never put together a words-and-pictures package and only then look for a magazine to take it on. Submitting an article speculatively is not much favoured these days, particularly when a set of photographs is included. Even if you have been diligent with your market study and are confident about the kind of pictures the editor prefers, send a letter of enquiry first, possibly enclosing a page of 'thumbnail' photographs, if they have been scanned into a computer.

Describing the photographs which are available or sending a page of these 'thumbnails' with your query letter reduces the chances of being rejected because the editor anticipates that the article could be a problem to illustrate. It is also an idea to request a copy of the magazine's guidelines for contributors, which should include details of their picture requirements.

Illustrating an Article With Your Own Pictures

You will soon learn to recognize when an illustration has the quality to sustain a manuscript. Each photo you submit should be appropriate to the theme. A good test of a picture's value is to consider whether it is adequate as a photograph, even without a caption. Always take care in referring in the text of your article to a detail in a picture, as some may not be selected for publication. It is preferable to restrict any direct reference to an illustration to the accompanying caption.

Just as a writer develops a theme for an article or an angle for a news story, so the writer-photographer should plan additionally in visual terms, to ensure the appeal and impact of the illustrations – but as I have said, you must be familiar with the type of photography that is expected.

You must be single-minded when making a final choice of pictures for publication. Take care not to be influenced by memories of the prevailing circumstances when the shots were taken, such as a pleasing atmosphere or extraneous events, which are not apparent in the picture. You also need to guard against the article's theme becoming secondary to the value of the pictures for their own sake. According to the type of subject, the role of the pictures may be to enhance the text visually, to convey information, to establish location or to indicate scale. Ensure that they perform that role, and are not included just because they are good photographs.

The writer who is new to taking pictures for publication is unlikely to have suitable negatives, prints or transparencies on file, which means taking photos specifically for a feature. This underlines the importance of sending an enquiry to an editor before proceeding in order to avoid wasted effort. At the outset you will concentrate on taking pictures that are in focus and have well thought-out composition and straight horizons, all of which will establish a basis for improvement. Newcomers to writing are encouraged to write about what they know. Similar advice applies to photography. Moreover, as you progress, ideas will also be generated by your photography itself which can be exploited by writing words which support the pictures.

Obtaining Pictures from Other Sources

Illustrating an article with your own pictures means that you can create a words-and-pictures package according to your original plan. However, depending on the kind of subject, there are other sources you can use. Some large companies have a press office or public relations department which is willing to make photographs available, free of charge. This can be useful when you are writing about matters associated with their business. Organizations, too, can be helpful in this respect, especially if they receive favourable publicity from your article.

If you are writing about entertainers, photographs are sometimes available from their agent. But do not let that deter you from taking a camera and some of your own ideas for photographs to the interview. Although pictures supplied by public relations departments may help a photographic newcomer, your aim should be to produce your own illustrations, for which you will receive a reproduction fee and an acknowledgement of your photography.

Before you have fully developed your picture-taking skills, there may be situations where you want to have control over the illustrations but feel you are too inexperienced to take them yourself. An option then is to find a good freelance photographer who is prepared to share the load. Or you could contact the secretary of a local camera club, who might be able to put you in touch with a competent enthusiast willing to assist with your projects on a regular basis. Working with a photographer may also be worth considering if you have plans for an illustrated non-fiction book.

Before coming to an agreement on this kind of collaboration, ensure that there is complete understanding on both sides. It is also advisable to see examples of the photographer's work before you proceed. You can simplify the financial side by asking the editor to pay for the manuscript and photographs separately.

If you are looking for a particular picture to illustrate an article, you could approach a picture library, but you should first request details of its rates. Consider such details as reproduction fees, service charges, search fees, the period of time the picture is required, costs for world rights, etc. One library's rates may be different from another's, so do not presume that there is a standard rate. Be particularly aware of clauses relating to damage or loss of material, and if you are involved in transactions between a picture library and a magazine or a publisher, ensure that the latter has adequate insurance to cover any mishap.

Book Illustrations

An accumulation of photographs related to a particular topic might prompt an idea for an illustrated book on the subject. But how you proceed is likely to be determined by the sort of book you wish to write. A subject such as cookery, for example, really requires a studio set-up to photograph the preparation of food, so if you did find a gap in the market for a cookery book, the publisher would probably want to handle the photography.

When contacting a publisher with a proposal it is important to list the pictures you already hold. You should also have an idea of the number of pictures your book will require. And in all circumstances it is prudent to discover a publisher's response to your suggestions before setting out on an expensive undertaking (see chapter 4). A book proposal may be less attractive to a publisher if, for example, you are unsure about supplying some of the photographs which form a fundamental part of your project. Before taking on a book of this kind the publisher will need to consider the additional expense of back-up library pictures, with perhaps the services of a picture researcher as well.

Taking Notes With Your Camera

In addition to taking pictures to illustrate your writing, a camera can be invaluable for taking visual notes. Photographs shot years before can jog your memory and reveal forgotten information. Although writers of fiction do not have to be concerned about finding subjects for illustrations, pictures can be vital in assisting your recollections of places, moods, people and exceptional weather conditions.

When writing fiction which includes references to historical sites, photographs of the setting are often very informative. Details which may not have been apparent when you visited the place can be surprisingly prominent in a good photograph. The juxtaposition of buildings which have a part in your plot can be accurately described when you have a picture that you can refer to. Plaques and inscriptions provide confirmation of dates and facts about buildings and locations. A good close-up shot can be taken without fuss and save you the trouble of copying the details by hand.

Colour or Black and White?

Should you use colour or black and white film? Numerous advances have taken place in printing and production methods over the last decade, and colour pictures are used widely in national newspapers. More colour has also been introduced in magazines, but many general interest articles continue to be illustrated with black and white pictures.

Newcomers also often ask whether a magazine can reproduce monochrome illustrations from colour prints. The answer is yes. Nowadays few magazines and newspapers stipulate that origination must be black and white. The majority of publications will accept colour prints for subsequent black and white reproduction. If in doubt at the shooting stage, take everything on colour stock. Modern techniques and equipment enable magazines to obtain excellent black and white reproduction, given a good original, which must be sharp and display a good colour balance.

Up-to-date market study is an obvious way of confirming how the magazine you have in your sights uses colour. You can then prepare your contribution accordingly. Despite the relative ease of reproduction from colour stock, when sending a words-and-pictures package to a periodical that is published in black and white, it may be advisable to submit black and white originals. However, a phone call to the magazine's editorial office will clarify their preferences.

Colour Transparencies or Prints?

Another query that is often raised is: if you are shooting in colour, is it better to use transparency film, and if so, is

35 mm satisfactory? For most publications 35 mm is acceptable; only a few companies, mainly producers of calendars and greetings cards, express a preference for a larger film size such as 6 × 6 cm. Until you are familiar with the various requirements, the easiest course to follow is always to check with your intended publisher first.

Film emulsions, materials and techniques are continually being improved, yet at the present time most publishers who use colour continue to prefer transparencies for colour reproduction. However, if big enlargements are not needed the majority of magazines will accept colour prints provided the quality is acceptable.

Processing Laboratories

Although a darkroom is an asset for an established writer-photographer, developing and printing can be a turn-off for some writers, who feel that getting involved in processing will eat into their precious writing time. Happily, there are excellent alternatives for those who prefer to keep out of the darkroom. The major consideration is choosing the most convenient and efficient service for your way of working.

Most high street processing shops are set up for colour only, so it is important to find a professional photo laboratory – check Yellow Pages – which can also provide a black and white service when it is required. An alternative to black and white film processing is to use chromogenic film (see chapter 5) and let the likes of Boots process it in C-41 chemistry.

If you cannot find help locally, it is worth looking through the classified advertisements of current copies of photography magazines such as *Amateur Photographer* for processors specializing in black and white. Various services are available including, for example, the reproduction of black and white prints from colour negatives.

Black and white developing and printing is normally more expensive than its colour counterpart. Instead of having a 35 mm film processed and all the negatives printed to 6 in × 4 in, it might be better to have the negatives contact printed on to a 10 in × 8 in sheet. You then have a proof of the entire film with the pictures reproduced the same size as the negatives, and can compare the results and, with the help of a magnifying glass, decide which shots should be enlarged.

Using a Camera Regularly

As a newcomer to photography it is unlikely that you will have a picture file. Using a camera regularly helps you establish your own collection of photographs. Even if you are shooting for a particular article, if there are more subjects than you envisage using, continue to capture them. Apart from obtaining a wider selection of material for the work in hand, you may end up with enough photographs to accompany another article, with a different slant.

Look upon each photo session as an assignment and never be miserly with film. There is little advantage in being economical with the number of exposures you take, if you have to do a reshoot because of a limited choice of images. Never forget that whenever pictures are surplus to your immediate needs they are valuable in building up your own source of illustrations.

If your experience of photography is restricted to little

more than shots of family occasions, make a start by trying to illustrate a current project which requires pictures. If the results are not good enough, the article can still be submitted; provided you did not promise the editor photographs, you will not have let anyone down. It is important not to commit yourself to a words-and-pictures package unless you are certain you are able to supply the photographs. If you fail to fulfil your commitment, you are unlikely to receive further commissions. So until you have gathered a reasonable number of pictures and feel confident enough to tackle most subjects, do not include pictures in your proposal to an editor.

As you become more competent, cuttings or tear sheets of your work will confirm that you are a published writer-photographer and give support to any proposal. So when your articles are published, obtain photocopies. They are ideal for editors who are not acquainted with you as evidence of your standard of work.

Photographs which are unmistakably related to the text can help an article or news story, and writers who produce their own illustrations have the advantage of ensuring a thematic continuity, which is sometimes lacking with loosely associated images. A words-and-pictures package which reads well and has the benefit of appealing visually is not only personally satisfying, but is more likely to be accepted for publication.

The more accustomed you become to taking pictures according to a precise brief, the more you will discover personal preferences for certain subjects. Whether your favourite types of pictures are artefacts, buildings or people, your files will soon reflect the categories of photography you prefer.

Specializing

As you discover these preferences, you may find your output directed towards markets that you have hitherto overlooked, and your accomplishments may encourage further progress, to the point of specializing. Do not scorn being recognized for a particular subject. It encourages editors to approach you when they require a feature on your speciality. On the other hand, do not over-specialize, as you could be out on a limb if that market dries up.

One word of warning: as a newcomer, do not think you can emulate the large colour spreads of cars and fashion. Photography of this type is usually organized by manufacturers' publicity departments and is often studio produced.

Relevant Images

Photographs are not pictorial accessories chosen simply to appear snugly alongside an expanse of type matter. If they are to be significant, the illustrations should be planned in conjunction with the article outline. When choosing the most appropriate photographs to illustrate your words, you should not be influenced entirely by personal preference. Select the most relevant images, following the information you acquired from your market study. It is always sensible to use a good conventional shot rather than a favourite experimental picture that has not achieved the intended purpose. Only submit photographs which will pass the closest scrutiny.

Whether you are writing for a specialist or a general interest periodical, photographs have an important part to play in getting your work published. An editor will consider your submission favourably because the article is more appealing with illustrations. Provided the pictures are technically good and relevant they will add an impressive dimension to the text.

Although the rates charged by picture agencies may give the impression that any shot which is published will earn a lot of money, rates of payment for pictures published can vary considerably. Most magazines have a set rate, which will usually be in addition to the sum received for the text. Some, however, pay a flat fee for a complete package of words and pictures. There will also be occasions when the payment for your photographs will be higher than that for your writing.

There is a tremendous feeling of elation when your manuscript and photographs are accepted for publication, followed by the work appearing in print and the cheque for your fee arriving through the letter box. Illustrating your manuscript with photographs can double your chances of getting published and increase the total payment for the feature.

2

Cameras, Accessories and Films

A camera That is Right For You

Choosing a camera from a vast array of similar-looking models can be a bewildering experience. And for writers who want to take up photography without the hassle of working out exposure, apertures and shutter speeds, there are many easy-to-use models available. During the last few years the 35 mm compact has transformed the camera scene, and there are compact cameras which can produce the quality of pictures that will complement your writing.

Compact Cameras

These days practically all compacts have auto-focus. Zoom models are also available, enabling the photographer to bring the subject closer and frame a shot precisely without having to change position. Auto-exposure, fill-in flash – to ensure that backlit subjects do not suffer from underexposure – red-eye reduction, and motorized film advance are included as standard by the majority of manufacturers.

Electronic information display panels and programmed

control are further examples of current technology. When choosing a camera from two or more models of comparable design and similar specifications, the deciding factor is often something like which one feels most comfortable to handle or whether the viewfinder is of a size which can be used with ease by a wearer of spectacles.

Although compacts at the cheaper end of the price scale will give acceptable results for general purposes, a camera with a choice of features will extend your scope and be more versatile for producing pictures suitable for publication.

A few compacts in the lower price range have a fixed-focus lens, which is designed to reproduce images which look sharp both at a distance and reasonably close. The lens is set in a single focus position, with the zone of focus extending from approximately 5 ft to infinity; the best pictures tend to be of subjects positioned about 12 ft from the camera. This can be thought of as a single focusing step, whereas an autofocus system has a series of steps. This system automatically locates the subject and focuses on the step nearest to it, to produce a photograph that is really sharp.

If you are looking for an automatic camera that is dependable and will produce good photographs in general situations, then a 35 mm compact model, perhaps with a zoom lens, could well be suitable for your requirements.

APS Models

As well as compacts for 35 mm, there are also Advanced Photo System (APS) models. APS uses a smaller film size – the actual image area is 30 mm × 17 mm, whereas the 35 mm format has an image size of 36 mm × 24 mm. APS models incorporate several features which are not available on 35 mm film cameras. Before deciding on an APS model, ensure the camera has the extras you require; some of the new hi-tech additions are to be found only on the more expensive cameras.

One of the features of APS cameras is drop-in loading. There is no film leader to fumble with; instead the film cassette slots into a small chamber in a similar way to inserting a battery. Four indicators on the film cassette show whether the film is unexposed, partly exposed or fully exposed or has been processed. Some cameras will also allow mid-roll change of film, permitting you to switch a partly used film for one of a different type and expose the remaining frames at a later date.

You can select the format of the final print when taking the picture. APS cameras offer three different print sizes: (C) classic 6 in × 4 in, the standard size print for 35 mm, normally produced by high street processors – to achieve this size the negative is cropped each side; (H) high-definition TV 7 in × 4 in, a print of similar proportions to a wide-screen TV image – the photograph is printed from the whole negative; and (P) panoramic 10 in × 4 in, which is an enlargement from the central portion of the negative.

The back of APS film is coated with a magnetic strip on which the exposure data is recorded. The information can be 'read' by the processing machine to enhance print quality. The date, frame number and even a short caption can be printed on the reverse of each photograph. After the film has been processed, the negatives are placed into the original cartridge, which is returned with a reference index print displaying all the pictures in thumbnail form. Also indicated are the negative numbers and the print format you selected.

To compensate for the smaller negative size, manufacturers introduced films with improved sharpness and grain structure to achieve results that would be comparable in quality to 35 mm film. The advances that have been made in film emulsion technology for the APS system are now also benefiting 35 mm film. Another APS feature which has also reached users of 35 mm film is the photo index print. When launched, the APS system was geared to the compact camera market, but single-lens reflex (SLR) models are also available.

For the novelist who wants a point-and-shoot camera to use as a picture notebook, an APS compact camera is the answer. It is ideal for capturing locations or specific detail as a visual record of information for a piece of fiction. Although the choice of three print formats can give variety to your results, bear in mind that the H size (7 in × 4 in) is the one which is printed from the whole negative.

While the APS system has many innovations, for the writer intending to take pictures for possible publication, a compact camera which uses 35 mm film size is a better choice because the larger film means that bigger and better quality enlargements can be made. However, if more control and flexibility are required, a 35 mm SLR camera should be considered.

35 mm Single-Lens Reflex (SLR) Cameras

Non-SLR cameras have a viewfinder that is independent from the lens, whereas with an SLR you view the subject through the lens by means of a mirror angled to reflect the image to the viewfinder screen. This means that you see exactly what the lens sees, whether the view is wide-angle, normal, telephoto or close-up. This is especially advantageous for sports photography or when you need to frame a subject near to the camera precisely.

The extensive range of 35 mm SLRs includes auto-focus

models, which are ideal for capturing moving subjects, and manual models for those who prefer to maintain complete control of focusing. However, a lot of auto-focus SLRs have a facility which permits manual operation for focusing adjustments and complete override as well.

Apart from auto-focus, many 35 mm SLRs have an extensive range of features including sophisticated exposure metering, built-in flash, easy-to-read digital information panels and programmed aperture and shutter speeds. Aperture priority allows you to choose the aperture setting (controlling the depth of the zone of focus) – the camera will automatically select the shutter speed to give the correct exposure. Similarly, shutter priority mode lets you decide on the shutter speed (controlling the degree to which the shutter 'freezes' the image) and the camera sets the aperture.

Medium-format Cameras

Cameras using 120 size roll film fall into the medium-format category. In addition to cameras with a standard format of 6 cm × 6 cm, other models give negative sizes of 6 cm × 7 cm and 6 cm × 4.5 cm. The 6 cm × 6 cm is a popular format with wedding photographers and for work in the studio. It is also used by photographers who take pictures for magazine covers and who supply stock transparencies to picture libraries.

The square format of 6 cm × 6 cm (56 mm × 56 mm in reality) gives valuable extra detail for pictures that are to be reproduced in very large sizes. There is an impressive quality about the negatives and transparencies produced by medium-format models. However, unless you plan to specialize, and your type of photography will eventually require 6 cm × 6 cm colour transparencies, a 35 mm format should be quite satisfactory for the pictures you need. A 35 mm outfit also weighs less.

Apertures, Shutter Speeds and Exposure

For those who prefer to let the camera look after exposing and focusing, an automatic camera is the model to choose. For those with manual cameras who have never come to terms with apertures, shutter speeds and exposure, then the following may be helpful.

The aperture and shutter speed settings on your camera allow you to control just how much light will fall on the film. The size of the aperture determines the volume of light which passes through the lens and the shutter speed controls the length of time it is allowed to do so.

Shutter speeds are arranged so that the exposure is halved when you change to the next fastest speed, or doubled when you change to the next slowest speed. For example, if the range of speeds read 30, 60, 125, 250 the time for which the shutter is open will be 1/30, 1/60, 1/125 and 1/250 of a second respectively (there are, however, normally more speeds than this).

The apertures or f-stops are arranged so that the exposure is halved when you change to the next highest aperture and doubled when you change to the next lowest aperture, provided the shutter speed remains constant. In other words if the aperture scale is marked f5.6, f8, f11 and f16, we know that f8 will admit half as much light as an aperture of f5.6, but twice as much as f11.

Combining the two, exposure of 1/30 second at f16 allows through the same amount of light as 1/125 second at f8. (The range of speeds and aperture settings vary according to the camera model.) By changing apertures or shutter speeds based on the camera's exposure reading or a separate exposure meter, you can select the shutter speed of your choice and obtain the correct exposure by adjusting the aperture and vice versa. The majority of cameras have a built-in light meter and SLR cameras measure light that passes through the lens.

Depth of Field

If the important aspect of a photograph is to freeze movement or action, selecting a fast shutter speed is the first consideration, and the aperture should be adjusted accordingly to obtain the correct exposure. A fast shutter speed and a large aperture would also be the choice if you were using differential focusing and setting the camera controls to give minimum depth of field. This technique should show the subject sharply depicted, with the rest of the scene out of focus.

The depth of field is the area which is in focus behind and in front of the point on which the lens is focused. When you wish to increase the depth of field (the area which is acceptably sharp) choose a smaller aperture. Remember that the closer the camera is to the subject, the shallower the depth of field.

Some SLR cameras have a depth of field preview button which, when pressed, stops the lens down and allows you to view the scene through the aperture selected to take the picture. This enables you to check the area of sharpness in the picture. Most lenses have a depth of field scale which indicates the zone of sharpness.

Lenses

The value of using an SLR camera is the interchangeability of lenses, which allows the photographer to select the most suitable for the job in hand. However, if you decide an SLR is for you and choose an expensive camera body, do not fall into the trap of trying to compensate by buying a cheaper lens. Always aim for the best lens you can afford. And never purchase additional lenses unless you really need them. If you have a camera with a standard lens, discover exactly what it is capable of producing before you consider buying others.

If you decide that additional lenses are essential for flexibility, it is not necessary to purchase several to cover every possible eventuality. For example, two useful lenses to complement a standard lens would be a 28 mm wide-angle and a 75-150 mm zoom. If you have more than one lens, ensure that any lens not being used is protected with a front and rear lens cap.

Standard

The focal length of a lens is measured in millimetres. A lens with a focal length of 50 mm is regarded as the standard lens for the 35 mm format (film area: 36 mm × 24 mm). Its angle of coverage gives a perspective rendition near to that of the human eye, and it gives results which are considered to be normal view for subjects, whether they are informal portraits of people or landscapes.

Wide-angle

Lenses of focal lengths shorter than 50 mm come into the wide-angle category. A wide-angle lens has a broad angle of view and a small image magnification. From an identical position a wide-angle lens will reduce the size of the subject and include more of the surroundings than a 50 mm. The background will also appear to be farther away.

Wide-angle lenses are very useful when you are taking pictures in a confined space, where it is imperative to include the maximum area in the picture. A wide-angle lens with a focal length of 28 mm or 35 mm is likely to be of most use to a writer-photographer. Results from lenses with a greater angle of view, known as ultrawide, can appear to be too exaggerated.

Telephoto

Telephoto lenses have a longer focal length than 50 mm standard ones and have a large image magnification but a narrower angle of view. As the focal length increases, so the image is magnified and far-off objects are brought closer. However, the depth of field, that is the area in which everything is acceptably sharp, looks shallower. This kind of lens is also ideal for isolating a subject from its surroundings.

Telephoto lenses are excellent for sports and wildlife photography. Focal lengths generally range from 85 mm to 300 mm, but longer lenses are available. Much depends on the kind of photography undertaken. A 135 mm lens is a popular choice. When you use a telephoto lens accurate focusing is essential; unless a fast shutter speed is selected, a tripod should usually be used to avoid camera shake and blurred images. As a general guide the slowest shutter speed that can safely be hand held will have similar numerals to the focal length of the lens being used. For example, select 1/60 as the slowest shutter speed for a 50 mm lens, 1/125 for a 135 mm lens and 1/250 for a 200 mm lens.

Zoom

It is possible to purchase a camera body and choose a lens other than a standard 50 mm. New models are often introduced with a zoom lens fitted. A zoom offers the attractive option of one lens with a range of focal lengths. It also provides the facility of framing a picture precisely without changing the camera position. This is an advantage especially when taking shots of sport or wildlife. If you prefer the minimum of equipment, an SLR with a 28–80 mm zoom could be adequate for your requirements.

Zooms come in wide-angle, mid-range and telephoto varieties. Popular among wide-angle zooms is the 24–50 mm; among mid-range types, 35–70 mm and 28–80 mm; and in telephoto, 70–150 mm and 70–210 mm. Some lenses in the tele-zoom category have a macro setting which allows you to get close when focusing on flowers or small objects.

Macro

Macro lenses are specially made for close-up photography. Several focal lengths are available, ranging from wide-angle to moderate telephoto versions. A common focal length is 50 mm. Macro lenses can be focused from infinity down to extremely close distances. Depending on the focal length, most macro lenses focus down to 1:2, giving a film image that is half life-size. There are also macro lenses which produce life-sized images – 1:1 ratio.

Buying Second-hand

If you have set your sights on a specific camera but find that it is too expensive for your budget, buying second-hand is a good alternative. Cameras which have been discarded in favour of the latest systems can often be found among the second-hand stock of photographic stores. If you buy a used model from a reputable photographic dealer, it will be approximately 30 per cent below the cost of its new equivalent, and you will know that it has been checked and tested and have the assurance of a guarantee lasting between three months and a year.

Another way of obtaining a used camera is to search the 'for sale' columns of photographic magazines. Dealers specializing in second-hand cameras also advertise in these magazines and back up their mail order service with a guarantee. Purchasing privately can be cheaper, but you will not get a guarantee. The terms used to describe second-hand cameras are usually as follows:

- *mint condition:* signifies the camera cannot be distinguished from new
- *excellent condition:* means the camera has been cared for, but signs of use exist
- *good condition:* suggests the equipment has been well used, but is not damaged

Some advertisements indicate the condition of cameras by grading them mint, mint–, excellent++, excellent+, etc.

Decide on a price range that is right for you, then look around for the camera that is going to be most suitable for your needs. Although a second-hand model is unlikely to be spotless, it is wise to examine any camera for signs of rough use. Check that the body is not badly scuffed and the lens is not scratched, and look for any corrosion or signs of leakage in the battery compartment.

Examine the camera back and make sure it opens and

closes smoothly and fits securely. While you have the back open look at the film guide rails for dents or marks which could prevent the film remaining flat. Check the condition of the pressure plates. Look at the shutter curtains/blades for any signs of damage. Wind the camera, still observing the condition and movement of the shutter, and feel whether the winding mechanism seems smooth.

Look through the viewfinder and check that the focusing screen is free from scratches. If the camera has an LCD display panel, make sure it is in good order. On SLRs examine the lens mount and ensure it is not excessively worn, and while doing so, look at the reflex mirror for signs of scratches or fingerprints.

Even a model of mint appearance could conceal faulty electronics so run a film through the camera as soon as possible on a variety of subjects and inspect the results. The same advice, incidentally, applies to a new camera. If the test pictures are satisfactory, the next step is to get to know the camera's capabilities and limitations.

As I have said, these days most cameras have a built-in light-metering system. If you buy a second-hand camera without a built-in meter, it is worthwhile purchasing a hand-held meter to measure the light and provide the exposure settings for your camera.

Flashguns

Just as compact cameras are equipped with a built-in flash facility, so too are some auto-focus SLRs. If you do not have a built-in flash or require a more powerful flash, there is a wide choice of flashguns available. 35 mm SLRs usually have a hot shoe fitting at the top the camera, but some flashguns can also be operated off camera for angled illumination. Another variation is reflecting flash off the ceiling or wall, referred to as bounce flash, for a softer effect. Bouncing the flash from a coloured surface is likely to cause a colour cast over the subject if you are using colour film.

Most of today's flashguns can be operated in auto or manual mode. When used manually, many flashguns may be fired at either maximum power or with reduced output. The photographer sets the aperture on the camera by hand according to the flashgun's guide number (power level) and the flash-to-subject distance. A flashgun usually has a table on the back displaying aperture and distance settings for various film speeds.

With some auto-exposure flashguns the aperture remains constant when set in auto mode and the flash output is cut off when a sensor on the flashgun determines that the subject has received sufficient light. This allows the photographer to concentrate on giving full attention to picture arrangement. Remember, the flashgun will take longer to recharge between pictures when the batteries are not fresh.

Also available are 'dedicated' flashguns which are intended to be used with specific cameras. It is important to be aware that flash can also be a boon when it is used as a fill-in facility for combating shadows on people in harsh sunlight and to overcome under-exposure with backlit subjects.

Lens Hoods

Whether you are protecting a lens from stray light outside the field of view or shooting into the light for a special effect, a lens hood is a very practical accessory. Although modern lenses are coated to reduce the problem of flare, if the rays of the sun hit the front of a lens the dazzling light is likely to spoil the picture.

If you are caught without a lens hood, improvise by shielding the lens from flare-producing light with the shadow of your hand. If this is not successful try an alternative viewpoint. To prevent damage to your eyes, never look at the sun through your viewfinder.

Tripods

A tripod is invaluable when a firm camera support is required. The majority are light to carry yet rigid when in use. They are useful for slow shutter speeds, time exposures and night-time photography. They are also an advantage when you need to keep the camera in the same position for an extended period.

When your camera is mounted on a tripod for a long exposure, a cable release will prove its worth in helping you avoid camera shake. Ensure that it works freely when you press the plunger, otherwise the vibration transmitted to the camera could cause the very camera shake that a cable release should help prevent. If your camera does not have a cable release fitting, you can still fire the shutter without touching the camera at the time of exposure by setting the delayed action mechanism to trip the shutter instead.

Filters

Accessories can be valuable in extending the scope of your

photography, but try to keep them to a minimum. There is little advantage in filling a camera bag with accessories if there is hardly any chance to use them. Filters, however, come into the useful and easy-to-carry category.

Made of dyed glass or plastic, they are obtainable in two shapes: one is circular with a holder that screws into a special thread on the front of a lens; the other is square and slides into a holder that is attached to an interchangeable adaptor. The benefit of the latter style is that if you change your camera or obtain an additional lens which takes a different size of filter, you need only buy another adaptor.

When using filters, your exposure should be increased as recommended by the manufacturer in order to compensate for the filter's density, which reduces light transmission. One filter which does not require an increase in exposure is a skylight filter, which is used with colour film. It absorbs excess ultra-violet light and reduces blue colour cast in photographs taken under a clear blue sky. It is a good choice for scenes near the coast and distant landscapes.

A UV/haze filter also does not require increased exposure. It is suitable for both black and white and colour film. The filter absorbs excess ultra-violet light but does not add warmth to colour film, which makes it suitable for high altitudes and snow scenes. Both skylight and UV filters also help to protect the lens.

A useful set of filters for colour films is the 81 series. They are made in a range of strengths and add warmth to an image. They also reduce the bluish cast caused by shade and overcast conditions. When using these filters it is worthwhile taking a shot without a filter for comparison purposes.

Filters which balance the light when used with a specific colour film are known as colour conversion filters. The 80A (blue colour) enables you to take photographs with daylight film in artificial light. The 85B (orange colour) permits you to use an artificial light film in daylight.

Other filters for use in artificial light that are worth keeping in mind are FL-D and FL-W. These correct the colour cast of 'daylight' or 'warm white' fluorescent lighting. Also available are effects filters such as starburst, diffuser, fog, etc., which can be considered for certain situations but need to be used sparingly. If they are overused the effects can become too commonplace. It is wise to experiment with any filter before using it on an assignment.

For black and white photography, filters lighten objects of similar colour and darken those of a complementary colour. Therefore, a yellow filter will darken blue and is ideal for giving a little extra emphasis to clouds. An orange filter will lighten yellow and red, darken blue and accentuate clouds more than a yellow one. It will also subdue freckles in portraits. A red filter will give dramatic cloud effects. A green filter will darken blue and red, and is very useful if you need to lighten fields and the foliage of trees which appear too dark.

Another filter which can be used for both black and white and colour is a neutral density (ND) filter which reduces the amount of light entering a lens and reduces the overall exposure. It is not a filter likely to be used regularly, but it is helpful if you only have a very fast film in extremely bright conditions and require a slow shutter speed or a wide aperture.

A polarizing (PL) filter will reduce reflections from non-metallic surfaces such as glass, plastic, polished wood, water, etc. It will also increase the colour saturation of a blue sky. The filter is rotated to obtain the desired effect.

FILTERS FOR COLOUR PHOTOGRAPHY

Filter	Factor	Effect
Skylight	None	Absorbs excess ultra-violet light and reduces blue colour cast in photos taken under clear blue sky. Suitable for coastal scenes and distant landscapes.
UV/haze	None	Absorbs excess ultra-violet light as Skylight filter but does not add warmth to colour film.
Neutral Density	×2 ×4	Reduces the intensity of light without affecting colour balance or contrast (also suitable for black and white film).
Polarizing	×3	Subdues reflections from non-metallic surfaces such as glass, plastic, polished wood, water, etc. Darkens blue sky.
Conversion 80A Daylight to artificial	×4	Balances the light for daylight film to be used in artificial light.
Conversion 85B Artificial to daylight	×2	Balances the light for artificial light film to be used in daylight.

FILTERS FOR BLACK AND WHITE PHOTOGRAPHY

Filter	Factor	Effect
Light Yellow	×2	Darkens blue slightly. Gives emphasis to clouds by darkening blue sky.
Medium Yellow	×3	As above but more pronounced.
Yellow-Green	×2	Lightens yellow and green, darkens blue and red slightly. Suitable for landscapes and foliage.
Green	×3	Renders green lighter, darkens blue and red. Ideal for fields and trees which appear too dark.
Orange	×4	Lightens yellow and red, darkens blue, also darkens green slightly. Accentuates clouds and penetrates haze. Subdues freckles in portraits.

Red	×7	Lightens red and darkens blue and green. Gives dramatic cloud effects and penetrates distant haze.
UV/haze	None	Absorbs excess ultra-violet (also suitable for colour film). For high altitudes, seascapes and snow scenes.
Polarizing	×3	Subdues reflections from non-metallic sufaces such as glass, plastic, polished wood, water, etc.

NOTE: A filter factor of ×2 requires exposure to be increased by one f-stop, ×4 by two f-stops, ×8 by three f-stops. Filter factors of different makes may vary slightly from those listed above.

Equipment Care

It is essential to keep your camera and accessories as clean as possible. A soft lens brush, lens tissues and an anti-static cloth will help to keep dust, fingermarks and smears to a minimum. Always take great care when cleaning a lens surface. Look after filters and care for them as you would a lens. Ensure that they are always held by the edges and never leave a filter loose in your camera bag.

Try to avoid 'tramlines' – parallel scratches that run down the length of a processed film. Often the cause is either minute grit caught in the felt light trap on the film cassette opening or dirt on the pressure plate on the inside of the camera back. One way to offset the trouble is to keep the cassette in its container until you are ready to load it into the camera. It is also a good idea to examine and clean the pressure plate regularly. Any preventative measure that is taken to keep blemishes in the finished photographs to a minimum is well worthwhile.

Films

Having decided on the camera best suited to the pictures you want to achieve, you must consider what type of film to use. An extensive choice is available in colour, and black and white negative films for producing prints, and in colour transparency films, which are also referred to as reversal or slide films. Although it is not necessary to experiment with them all, be prepared to try more than one brand or speed of film until you are satisfied with the results.

Films are manufactured to cope with different photographic circumstances and can be divided into groups according to the speed (sensitivity to light) of the emulsion: slow, medium, fast and ultra-fast. Slow-speed films are usually the choice when optimum quality is required. Fast-speed films are not as fine-grained, but being more sensitive to light they require a shorter exposure than slow ones. This permits higher shutter speeds and smaller apertures which provide more depth of field.

The measurement of film speed is stated as an ISO (International Standards Organisation) rating. It comprises values equivalent to the old ASA (American Standards Association) and DIN (Deutsche Industrie Normen). For example, the ratings on a box of 400-speed film are usually given as ISO 400/27°. In general use the last figures (27°, the DIN rating) are usually dropped. The higher the ISO number the more light-sensitive is the film.

Slow-speed Film

Ratings include ISO 25, ISO 50 and ISO 64. Films in this group give excellent sharpness, detail and very fine grain –

the minute irregular clumps which comprise the developed image on the film.

Medium-speed Film

Ratings include ISO 100, ISO 125, ISO 160 and ISO 200. These are films to use in reasonable weather conditions and are recognized as fine-grain films.

Fast-speed Film

ISO 400 comes into this group. It has a wider exposure latitude than medium-speed film and is suitable for dull conditions and for photographing action. Thanks to the latest advances in film technology, grain is less discernible these days. ISO 400 colour negative films are vastly improved and can be considered to be in the fine-grain category. They are recommended as all-purpose films and are a good choice for compact camera users. Black and white negative films of ISO 400 rating are mostly regarded to be medium-grain.

A special group known as chromogenic films, manufactured by Ilford, Kodak and Konica, come into the fine-grain classification. They are nominally rated at ISO 400 but have a wide exposure latitude and give very fine-grain prints compared with other films of equivalent speed. They can be processed in universal colour chemistry C-41 at your local colour mini-lab, which is extremely convenient when you want the results in a hurry. This aspect, together with Ilford's XP2 Super black and white film, is considered in Chapters 5 and 7.

Ultra-fast-speed Film

This group ranges from ISO 800 and is for extreme low-light situations and very fast action photography. Other films in this group have speed ratings of ISO 1000 and ISO 1600, which give coarse grain and ISO 3200 which gives very coarse grain.

It should never be assumed that one make of film will give the best results in every situation, particularly in colour. Just as people differ in their appreciation of colour, so film manufacturers produce emulsions which represent their particular interpretations. Some films appear warmer overall, whereas others will give a subdued, cooler result. A certain film might be superb in bright conditions but respond poorly on a dull day. Therefore, it is worthwhile discovering the different qualities of films and which manufacturers' films are most suited to your type of photography and personal choice.

As to transparency films, those of a slow speed rating are usually the sharpest, but they need good lighting conditions. When the light is not good or you are trying to capture action, a faster film or supplementary lighting such as flash is required.

35 mm films for colour or black and white negatives can be purchased in cassettes of 24 or 36 exposures. APS films are available in 25- and 40-exposure cassettes. Colour transparency film is also obtainable in 24- or 36-exposure cassettes. Never be caught without film; always carry more than you think you will need.

Exposure Latitude

The current range of cameras includes many features designed to make photography as accurate and straightforward as possible, particularly as far as exposure is concerned. Colour negative films have a wider exposure latitude than colour transparency films. This means that if a picture is exposed incorrectly, the effect on the colour quality is not as significant with colour negative film as it is with colour transparency film. When there are minor exposure faults on colour negative film, the shortcomings can be rectified at the printing stage. Transparency film does not have this advantage, so it is important to get the exposure right. Any over-exposed transparency will have weak, washed-out colour, and this will usually ruin any hopes of publication of all but the most exceptional images.

One way to overcome this problem is by bracketing. This is a method used to achieve correct exposure when using transparency film in difficult situations, especially with backlit subjects or scenes of extreme contrast, such as sunlight filtering through trees. It means taking additional shots at an aperture stop or half-stop above and below the exposure setting indicated on the camera or exposure meter. The technique is also useful when you are confronted with an unrepeatable subject and it is vital you capture the best picture possible.

Uprating Film

If a situation requires a fast film and you only have a film of, say, ISO 100, you could try the method known as uprating the film. This is using a film of one ISO rating as a film of a higher rating. If you wanted to use an ISO 100 as ISO 200 you would simply adjust the ISO setting on the camera to ISO 200. This would uprate the film by one aperture stop. If you uprated by two stops, you would need to adjust the film setting on the camera to ISO 400. After exposing an uprated film it is necessary to find a professional laboratory, request push-processing, and inform the processor how much the film has been uprated. The term 'push-processing' means giving the film more development to compensate for the under-exposure caused by uprating the film.

Colour transparency and black and white films respond to uprating better than colour negative film (although some professional C-41 emulsions were designed for possible uprating). The overriding factor is that some image quality will be lost. Grain will become more noticeable, and there will be an increase in contrast and a loss of shadow detail. That is why the normal film rating on the box is the one to follow. Furthermore, not all laboratories offer a push-processing service.

Home processing is not possible with Kodachrome transparency film and it is necessary to send exposed films to Kodak laboratories, where only a minimum of push-processing is offered. So if you think you will need to uprate films, it is prudent to experiment first and then only with professional films. But a more satisfactory option is always to keep a spare fast film in your camera bag.

DX Coding

DX coding is a system that ensures that the correct ISO film speed rating is set each time you change a film. It is found on the outer metal of film cassettes in a pattern of black and silver. When a DX-coded film is used in a camera which has been designed to read the auto-sensing code on the cassette, the camera will automatically set the correct speed for its exposure system.

It should be noted that when DX-coded film is used in cameras without a film sensor, the film speed must be set manually. DX recoder self-adhesive labels are available for uprating films for use in DX film-loading cameras.

Digital Cameras

If you use a computer, you may consider purchasing a digital camera to provide your illustrations. Digital cameras certainly offer an alternative approach to obtaining photo images; photos are taken electronically, without the assistance of film.

A digital camera is operated in a similar way to a compact model. Some feature built-in flash, and most have an automatic exposure system, and a conventional viewfinder. There are also some digital SLRs. An LCD display screen enables you to examine the image you have photographed instantly, which means that if you are unhappy with the result you can take another shot immediately. But remember that using the LCD display screen instead of the viewfinder will shorten the life of the batteries.

When you press a digital camera's shutter release to make an exposure, instead of the image being recorded on film the light is directed at a charge-coupled device (CCD) chip, containing pixels. An electrical charge is created which is converted into a digital image. All things being equal, the more pixels a CCD comprises, the better the quality of the image.

Specification details of digital cameras usually state pixel values, which give an indication of the image quality that can be expected. Basic digital cameras produce images of approximately 350,000 pixels, but there are megapixel models of 2–3 million pixels which are nearer the starting point for 'photo quality' pictures to accompany your manuscripts. A further consideration in this assessment is the quality of the lens.

Images captured on a digital camera are stored in its memory, which will hold from four to a hundred images, depending on the resolution. The majority of cameras have an adjustable quality setting. Aiming for the best quality will reduce the number of images the memory can store. To assist storage, most digital cameras will accept additional memory cards which can be replaced when they become fully loaded. More than one type of card is available, which allows you to choose the most suitable for your requirements. After the images have been downloaded to your computer, the memory card can be wiped clean and reused.

Transferring Your Images to a Computer

Digital cameras are supplied with a cable which enables you to download images directly to a computer. Some have an infrared system that provides a cable-free connection to the computer. There are also some desktop printers which can be linked directly to a digital camera or will respond to a camera's memory cards so that photographs can be printed without having to download them to a computer.

However, most photographers are likely to prefer to view their digital pictures on a monitor before printing. Moreover, once downloaded, the images can be enhanced and manipulated in a number of ways. The colour balance can be altered, unwanted clutter can be removed, dust marks can be retouched, and in some cases the picture can be made sharper.

A variety of software packages such as Adobe Photo Deluxe are available to effect such improvements. Once the images have been adjusted, they are then ready to be reproduced on an inkjet printer. You can also send them around the world as e-mail attachments or upload them to your web site.

3

Taking and Making Pictures

Publishable Photographs

Photographs with creativity or impact will attract attention whether they are printed in a periodical or displayed on an exhibition wall. They will also be more likely to be accepted for publication, whether it is a matter of one or two black and white prints accompanying a short article or a complete set of colour transparencies forming part of a feature package.

Modern cameras are capable of achieving pin-sharp photographs at the touch of a button. The anxieties caused by trying to remember camera technicalities are no longer a problem. However, the vital function of composing a picture creatively still needs attention. A publishable photograph is the outcome of a number of variable factors, including viewpoint, lighting conditions, time of day and choice of lens. But the most important factor is how you perceive the subject and arrange the picture in the viewfinder.

To ensure consistent improvement in your photography,

examine each picture and decide whether you achieved the result you visualized when you pressed the shutter release. Identify the plus as well as the minus points and make a note of any changes which could be made in your approach on future occasions.

By maintaining an awareness of current trends in photographs published in magazines and newspapers, you will have a standard by which you can judge your own shots. This will be especially helpful when you are selecting pictures to blend with your written words. Whenever you are producing photographs for an article or a book, bear in mind that illustrations for creative writing require creative photography.

Making a Picture

At the moment of positioning a subject in the viewfinder, endeavour to 'make' rather than simply 'take' a picture. This approach will bring a recognizable improvement in your photographs. Making publishable pictures is about clearly composing your subject so that it fills the frame. It is necessary to get close enough so that whatever you are photographing dominates the picture area and competing interest is eliminated. An exception to this rule is when a picture is intended to be used as a cover picture. Tightly cropped images are unsuitable for magazine covers where the illustration bleeds on all edges (i.e. where it goes to the very edge of the page). In addition, space on and around the subject is often used for type matter highlighting the main features which are to be found on the inside pages.

Ensure that you are observing exactly what the camera is

going to record. Avoid being so preoccupied with the major components of a scene that you overlook broken fences, telegraph poles and litter. Often a slight alteration of the camera position will exclude extraneous details completely.

Creative Composition

When you set about framing your ideas in the viewfinder, always ask yourself whether the subject would have more impact in portrait rather than landscape format. Consider also whether the composition could be strengthened by moving the main subject to the left or right of the picture area. In most cases, placing the main subject off-centre will improve the composition and enable subsidiary subject matter to be arranged effectively in the frame. But in certain situations it may be necessary for the major feature to be located in the middle of the picture area for effect or perhaps to convey a sense of symmetry.

Even when you are pleased with your choice of viewpoint, do not expose all your shots from the same position; try alternative angles. Also, do not take every picture from eye-level while in a standing position; choosing a low vantage point, perhaps while kneeling, can transform a mediocre scene into a stunning photograph.

However hard you try, there will be occasions when the splendid image you remember capturing turns out not to be so outstanding after all. Your expectations may have been prompted by the surroundings, certain sounds or perhaps the fragrance of flowers which you noticed when you were looking through the viewfinder. Accept these situations and learn from them.

Visual Organization

Avoid positioning a tree or the horizon so that the picture area is split into equal halves, because this suggests divided interest and indecision. For a landscape or seascape it is preferable to position the horizon line approximately one third from the top or bottom edge of the frame. Normally this strengthens the composition, with the significant proportion of the scene being arranged in the higher or lower two thirds of the photograph.

If you are frustrated by a tree or a large obstruction spoiling your picture arrangement, remember that what you cannot move physically can be overcome by changing the camera's position and moving the obstacle optically.

Once you are satisfied with the position of the image you see in the viewfinder, ensure that the edge of the frame is free from distracting details protruding into the picture area. Give extra attention to each corner; make this part of your procedure before pressing the shutter release. Also keep a lookout for any litter spoiling the foreground. Removing an unwanted tin or a piece of paper can avoid unnecessary retouching on the final print.

A sound basis for a well-composed picture is to think of a photograph being divided into nine equal areas by two horizontal and two vertical imaginary lines. The four points where the lines intersect are considered to be the strongest parts of the composition, and you should try to position the main subject at one of those points.

This technique is often referred to as the rule of thirds, but I consider such 'rules' to be simply guidelines for logical picture arrangement rather than principles to follow without deviation. If by ignoring the rules on occasions a picture with appeal and impact can be achieved, then the final result justifies the method used. Remember, a camera is a tool which records your intention; composing the picture is down to you.

Lines and Shapes

Lines and shapes are distinctive elements in a photograph's make-up. By observing published photography you will discover line and shape in subjects of all kinds. Natural lines such as pathways or the curve of a river can be positioned to lead the eye into the picture. There are also lines which are formed by the edge of one tone or colour against another.

Lines also contribute to the mood of a scene. Horizontal lines imply tranquillity, whereas vertical ones suggest grandeur and power. Diagonal lines give a feeling of movement and speed. Curved lines attract attention. Shapes also catch the viewer's eye and can be used to strengthen a picture. Be aware of shapes formed by shadows, which can easily be overlooked in the viewfinder but may cause disappointment in the final result.

The quality of light is a substantial element in the composition of a photograph. Even direct sunlight differs with the seasons and time of day. At midday shadows are dense and the light appears harsh. When the sun is lower, shadows lengthen and need to be reckoned with in the overall composition. Oblique sunshine accentuates texture and detail.

Close-up Detail

If you want to show close-up detail or small items, you need to consider the size of the subject and how close your camera will focus. With many compact cameras you can get near enough to cope satisfactorily with subjects such as church pew-end designs, carved effigies and lecterns, and obtain good close-up photographs. These subjects can be illuminated by flash or, provided it is bright enough, available light.

Smaller objects like coins or medals, for example, will require a different approach. An SLR camera with a macro lens is ideal for this kind of close-up photography. If the available light is good, arrange the objects near a window. If you decide to shoot the pictures outdoors, try to avoid the strong overhead sunlight of midday, which will cause high contrast and dense shadows. A cloudy, bright sky is preferable.

Plain backgrounds are best. You can create your own with a large sheet of light-coloured card or thick paper. Arrange the objects to be photographed on one half of the card. Do not fold the card in half but carefully bend it so that it forms both a base and a background, and ensure that it shows no crease or fold.

Photographing People

Whether you are interviewing someone for a feature or a profile piece, photographs of your interviewee are going to give your words visual support when your manuscript is considered for publication. There will be occasions when an editor agrees to your proposal of a celebrity interview, but prefers to arrange for a photographer to obtain the pictures. This means that providing the illustrations is out of your control. When only a portrait shot is required, a recent photograph can sometimes be supplied by the interviewee.

Preparation

If you are handling the photography as well as writing the feature, ensure that the illustrations complement the overall coverage of the interview. Diligent preparation is the key. Planning your photographs with care and a creative approach will result in better pictures and increase the likelihood of getting them published.

When you make arrangements for the interview explain the type of photographs you hope to take. This will avoid the interviewee being surprised or unprepared on the day and will probably enable them to dress accordingly. It is also important to confirm how much time your subject can allow you. Listen to any suggestions the subject makes, but when the photography session starts, ensure that your instructions and requests are clear and that you politely control the situation.

Planning can take almost as long as the actual interview. In addition to arriving for an interview with conversation starters, a sequence of questions, and a list of picture ideas, have some idea of alternative photographs as a back-up should your original plans prove to be impractical.

First, seek to portray the personality of your subject. If the interview is conducted at the person's home, aim to include both indoor and outdoor shots, weather permitting. Some people are self-conscious when facing a camera. The rapport that is established during the course of the interview will be beneficial in putting your subject at ease when you start taking pictures. The best way of putting someone at ease is to appear relaxed yourself.

If people feel uncomfortable this will probably be apparent in the photograph, so take at least one or two shots of your subject in an easy chair, and be prepared to make adjustments to the pose. Although informal shots are the aim, remember that the eyes are a significant feature of a face so ensure that they are in sharp focus. If the hands appear awkward give the person something to hold. A position which permits them to support their chin with one hand can be satisfactory provided it looks natural and not contrived.

Try to ensure that you have a reasonable variety of poses on film. Get your subject to look out of a window, read a book or peruse correspondence, use a word processor, or stand in an open doorway. Be wary of backgrounds with intricate detail, such as heavily patterned wallpaper or curtains, which may be ideal for a picture of a room's decor but is distracting in a head-and-shoulders photograph.

Spontaneity

It is vital to achieve a feeling of spontaneity in your photographs. This can be accomplished by calling for your subject's attention immediately before firing the shutter. This is particularly good when children are being photographed, so ensure you are alert to seize the moment.

When using a camera requiring manual adjustments keep to a fail-safe routine by always setting the shutter-speed, aperture and focusing in the same sequence, followed by a final check in the viewfinder before you release the shutter. This should become an instinctive operation which allows you to concentrate on capturing the fleeting expressions of the person in your viewfinder.

Associating People with their Interests

Plan to take shots which associate your celebrity with his or her profession or leisure pursuits. Natural-looking results can be achieved if people appear to be absorbed in whatever they are doing. A link can also be made by using a familiar building as a backdrop, such as a theatre for an actress, a college for a professor, a church for a clergyman. If this sort of approach is not practicable, consider using a local landmark to identify your subject with the area. Careful attention to arrangements for outdoor photos of this type and the co-operation of the interviewee are essential.

Reducing 'Red Eye'

The majority of photographs taken indoors will be with the aid of flash, so beware of the problem known as 'red eye'. This is when the eyes of a person resemble a red glow in a colour photograph. This peculiarity is caused by the flashgun being very close to the camera lens and the flash being reflected off the retina at the back of the eye.

For users of SLR cameras the answer is to utilize an extension lead and position the flashgun away from the camera or to bounce the flash off the ceiling or a wall. But remember, if the surface is not white, it will introduce an overall colour cast in the pictures, as we saw in chapter 2. Compact cameras usually have built-in flash, but a number of models have a pre-flash system to reduce 'red eye'.

Available Light

Make time to try an informal portrait illuminated by available light from a window. For a head-and-shoulders shot taken this way a large sheet of white card or paper can be used as a reflector for directing light into shadow areas of the face.

If you take close-up pictures of your subject in a garden, avoid a backdrop of wire netting or a wooden trellis and, of course, the age-old mistake of a tree growing out of someone's head. Television aerials can be overlooked just as easily, so it is imperative to make a final check in the viewfinder.

Summer light can be dazzling and unflattering, especially when the sun is directly overhead. If you are taking an outdoor portrait and the high sun is causing the person to frown and squint, you could combat the problem by choosing a shady area and using a flash. If heavy shadows around the eyes and beneath the nose are the trouble, a sheet of white card or paper could be used to reflect light into those areas.

Taking photographs of a celebrity does not mean that a large display of equipment is required. Whether your camera is a compact or an SLR model, the essential point is that you should be completely familiar with its controls.

Using a Tripod

Take advantage of accessories that will help you to keep problems to a minimum. A tripod comes into this category when you are taking an informal portrait. Apart from reducing the chances of camera shake, you can move around and make adjustments, knowing that the camera position will remain constant.

A further benefit of a tripod is that you can look directly at your subject and have a conversation without struggling to keep an eye peering through the viewfinder. This makes for a more relaxed atmosphere while you attempt to capture the facial expression that is 'just right'. Above all, keep things simple and refrain from experimenting; a reshoot should be avoided.

Groups

Writers who already illustrate their articles are aware of the value of human interest in their pictures. But if a photograph includes a number of people, it is better if they are engaged in some form of activity. For a fishing village feature, a shot of fishermen mending their nets would be preferable to a static-looking shot of a deserted harbour at low tide.

When photographing a group of people, an informal arrangement can be more effective than a rigid line-up. This can be achieved by getting them to stand or sit at various levels. Ensure that the face of each person can clearly be seen. This is another case when, once you have everyone in place, a tripod will allow you to move around in the knowledge that the camera's position will not change. You can devote more attention to the group without having to refer to the viewfinder before firing the shutter release.

For groups it is advisable to make several exposures in order to increase the chance of getting a final result in which everybody appears reasonably attentive. When you are taking pictures of a group with a building with which the people are associated, position them carefully so that the group occupies a dominant area of the frame.

Photographing Buildings

Overcoming Distractions

Taking pictures of buildings, with or without human interest, embraces an extensive range of subjects from a thatched cottage to a contemporary shopping mall. Whichever category of illustration is required to complement your writing, your major aim is to present the building as effectively as possible.

Good light is high on the list of priorities for achieving the best possible results. Architectural detail which requires prominence in a published picture can be enhanced by certain lighting conditions. Choosing the time of day which offers the best direction of light can mean the difference between a mediocre shot and an outstanding one. The angled light of early morning or late afternoon can bring a building to life. A cityscape that appears mundane at midday can be transformed by directional light when the sun is low.

Texture, too, plays an important role in photographs of architecture. Details of stonework, wood and wrought iron are emphasized by side lighting. Coloured shapes, brick-work and geometric patterns are also enriched by angled light. Make use of shadows to accentuate line and shape.

When photographing public buildings or well-known land-marks, people can be a problem. Passers-by who appear prominently in a composition can create divided interest, especially when the architecture is the feature you wish to emphasize. Having said that there are occasions, of course, when a person may be deliberately included in a shot to convey scale, or may be necessary in the context of the picture.

A change in the angle of view can often eliminate bystanders from a photograph, but returning to a location at a different time of day is sometimes the only solution to getting a shot without people in the way. Unwanted details, such as parked cars, can be less conspicuous when in shadow, and others can sometimes be obscured by a low boundary wall or shrubs.

Historical Architecture

If your assignment requires photographs of a castle, manor house or stately home, first shoot some pictures of the entire building and its immediate surroundings. Once you are satisfied that you have a good record shot of the overall subject, you can then concentrate on the most effective features for the purpose of your article.

When working on historical buildings, research into the period or information from a guidebook can be helpful in discovering little-known details about the structure. Decorative stonework and timber are often important enough to be photographed in close-up.

A cluster of small buildings can appear mundane in a photograph because of the similarity of structure and size. This problem can be avoided by a precise selection of viewpoint and by giving emphasis to one or two of the buildings.

To arrive at a location and find a well-known landmark surrounded by scaffolding is a disappointment sometimes encountered by photographers. When it does happen, make the best of the situation by taking a few shots of the enveloped architecture for possible future use.

Contemporary Design

Office blocks of contemporary design with steel and heat-reflecting glass façades can be presented in a graphic manner. Images reflected in the mirror-like walls of modern structures can result in striking effects. Remember that any inscriptions or signs will appear reversed in reflections and in some instances it might be preferable to exclude them from the frame. Alternatively, if you want to reduce or remove such reflections, a polarizing filter should be used.

Any upward tilt of a camera to include the top of a building will cause the sides of the structure and vertical lines to converge in the picture. Anyone photographing architecture regularly will benefit from using a shift lens, which gives perspective correction control and enables the highest point of a building to be framed without vertical lines converging.

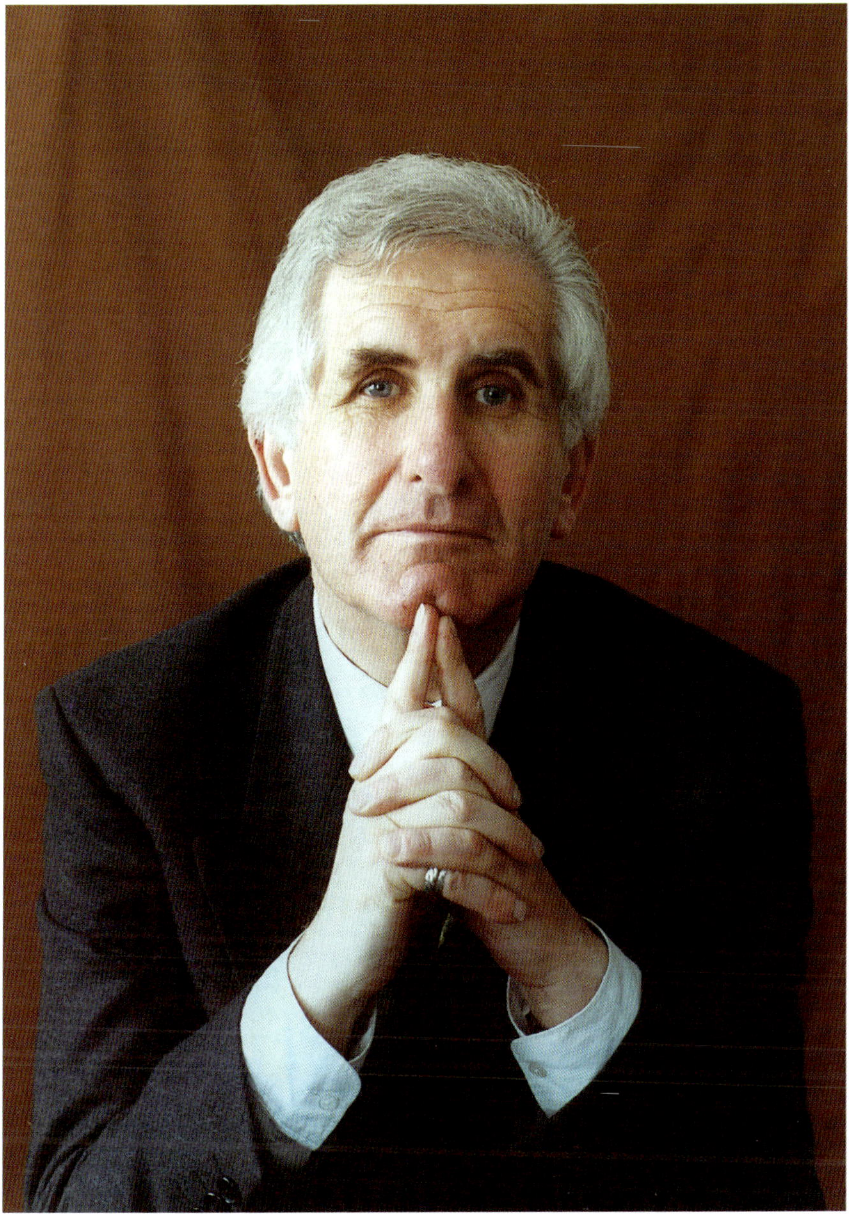

This portrait of poet and writer Phil Streeter is an example of making the most of available daylight from a large window. Phil was positioned so that the illumination came from the side. However, there was sufficient light to provide subtle modelling to the side of the face farthest from the window

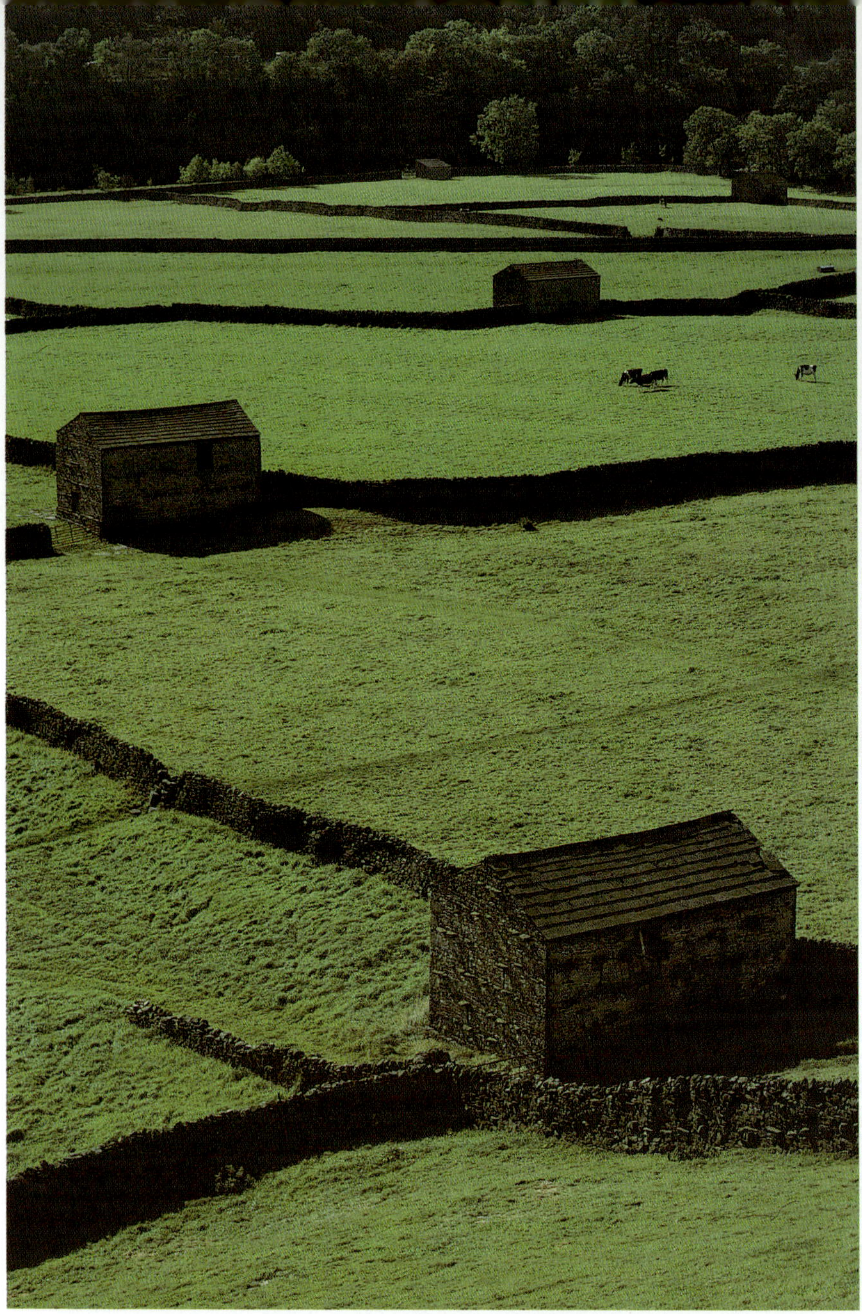

A graphic landscape in Swaledale, North Yorkshire. The pattern of the drystone walls and the small buildings combine to lead the eye into the picture. More often than not a successful photograph is the result of climbing a hill, waiting for the sun to break through or, in the case of the above shot, returning to the location when the weather was more favourable

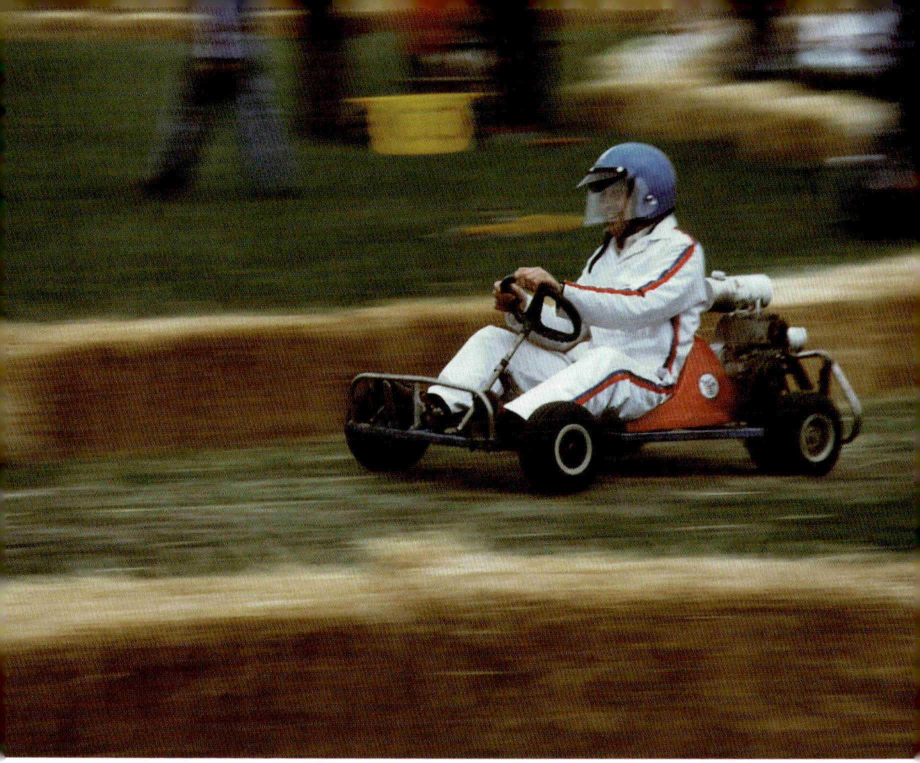

The basis of the technique known as panning is to convey an impression of speed by using a slow shutter speed and keeping a moving subject in the same position in the viewfinder during exposure. The go-kart was followed in the viewfinder well before the shutter was released and the tracking was continued smoothly until after the exposure was complete

To convey the vastness of this field of poppies, two-thirds of the frame was given to the blaze of colour. The shot illustrates the story of an Isle of Wight farmer who took the 14-acre field out of corn production and let it revert to chalk grassland. Poppies which had lain dormant for years burst into bloom and the rare sight attracted a number of artists

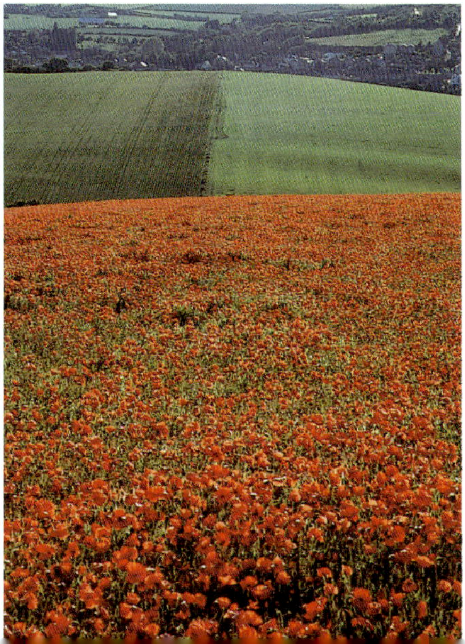

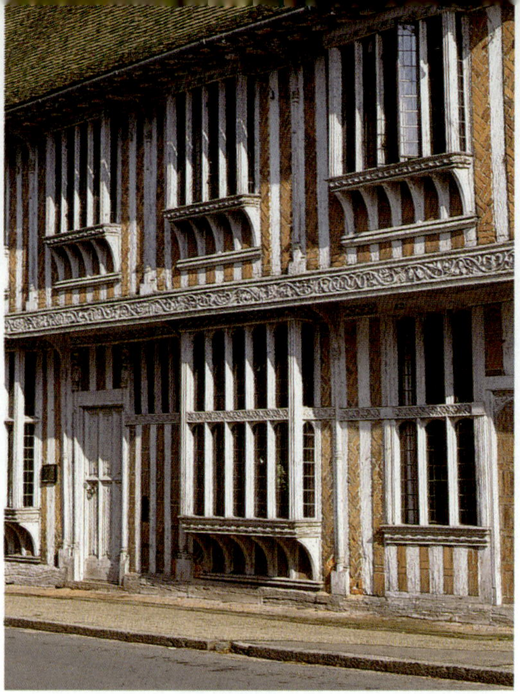

When you assess a building for pictures look for both prominent and secondary features. This splendid timber-framed sixteenth-century merchant's house has several facets which could be highlighted both in close-up and not so close photography. The rich carvings decorating the building reflect the family's success. The door has linen-fold panels and the carved frieze embellishes the entire frontage

A line-up of cockle boats moored near the shore could make an attractive scene as an establishing shot in a selection of illustrations. But a photograph of fishermen unloading their catch would impart the important ingredient of activity to the sequence of the pictures. Illustrations should not only enhance the text but also complement each other

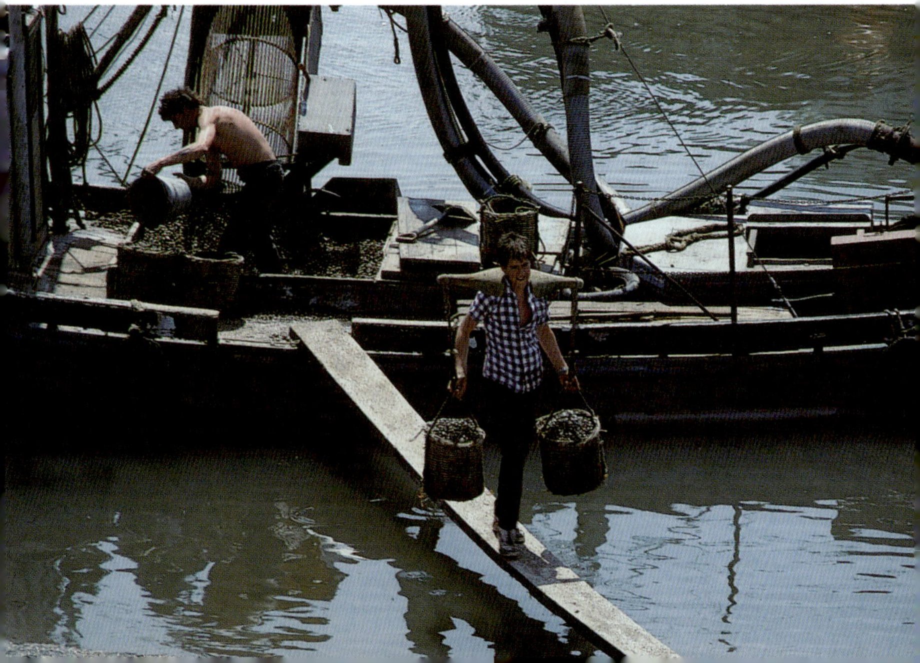

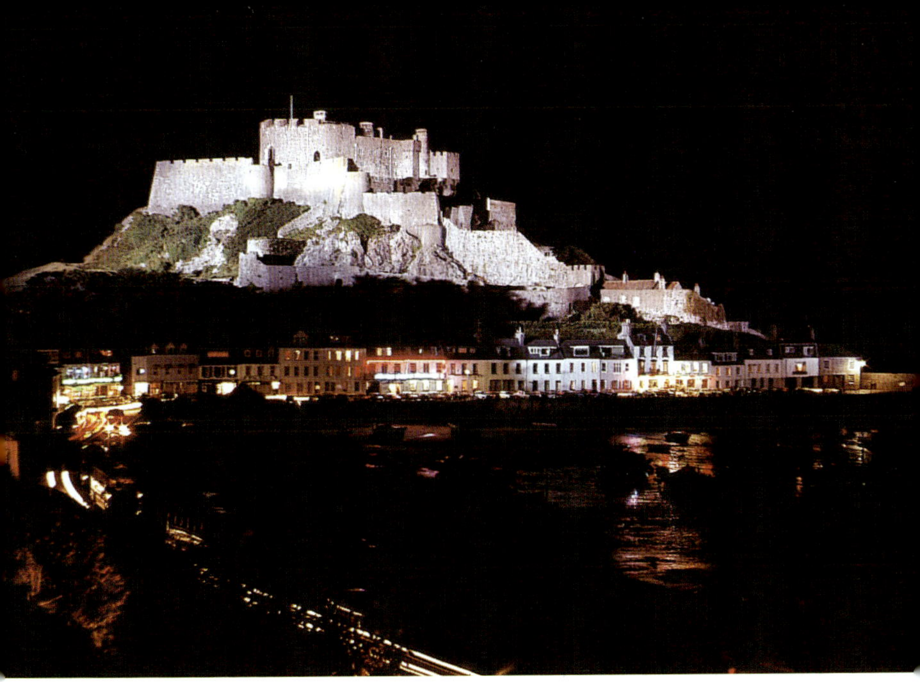

A night shot of Mont Orgueil Castle, Jersey, dramatically transformed by floodlighting. With night photography longer exposures are required, which makes the use of a tripod essential. If you are caught without a tripod, find a box or wall to support your camera. A cable release will help you avoid camera shake

You should take pictures from more than one viewpoint. This modern sculpture, representing the figure of Christ, is housed beneath a canopy over a church entrance. As well as photographing the entrance and canopy from a viewpoint which presented an overall perspective, the sculpture complete with shadows provided a more dramatic shot

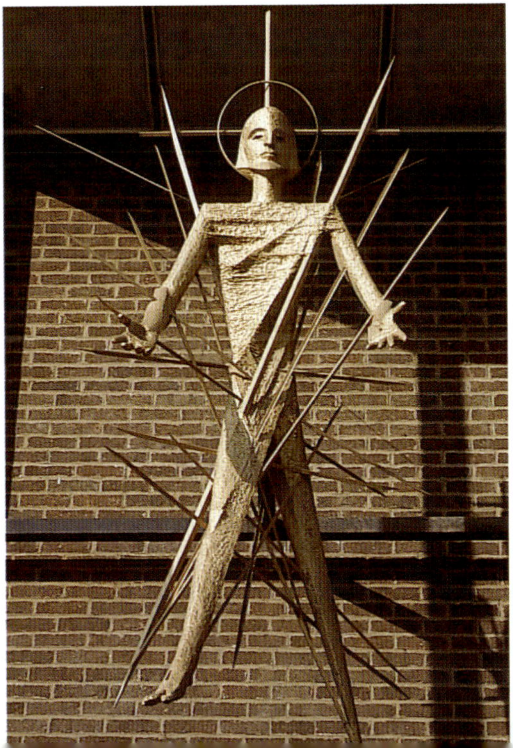

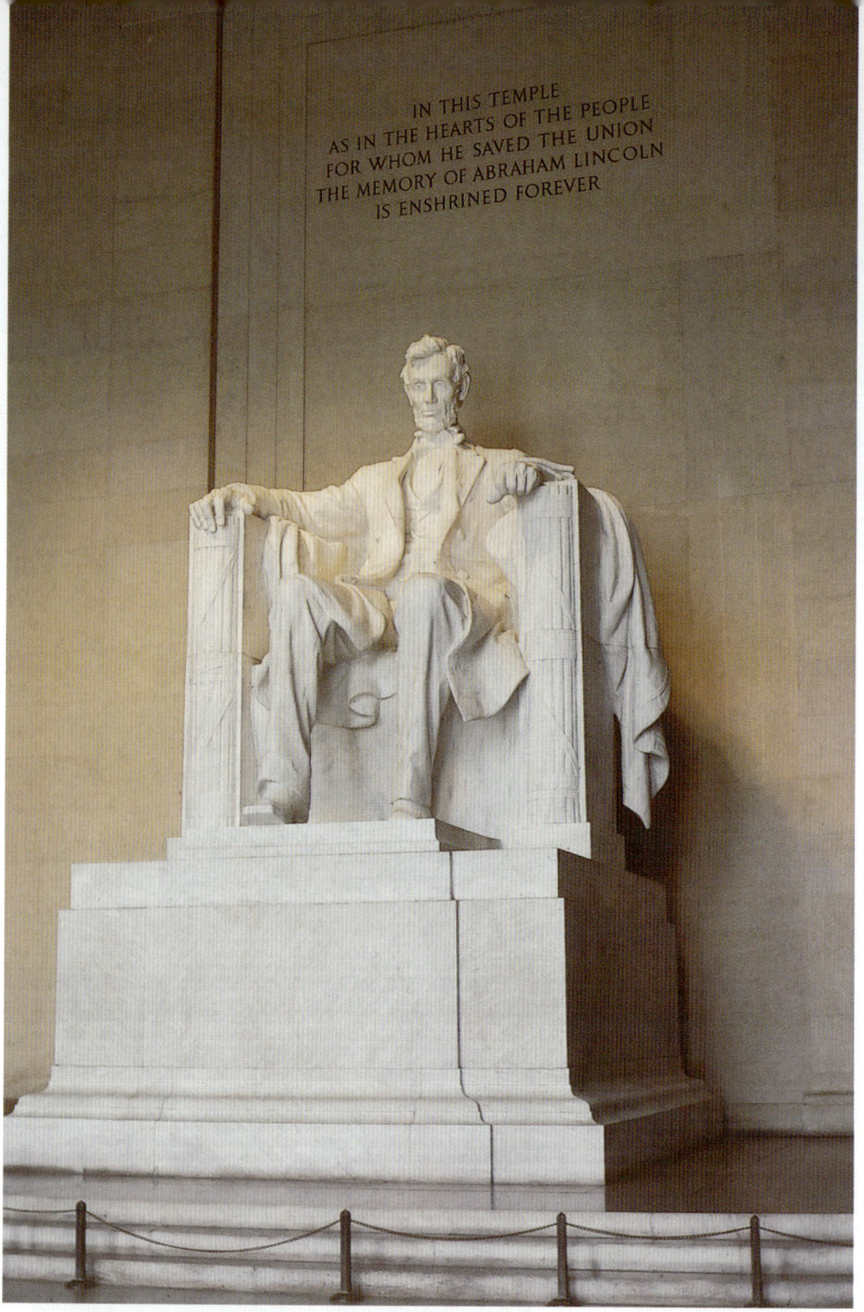

The Lincoln memorial building in Washington DC offers several viewpoints for photographing the notable statue of Abraham Lincoln. The many visitors who are attracted to this memorial make taking pictures without people in the way difficult. An early-morning visit enabled me to photograph the giant statue from the viewpoint I preferred

Humour is not the easiest of subjects to depict on film, yet the opportunist deer raiding the deer food dispenser suggests an amusing situation. When a humorous incident occurs it is advisable to take a shot immediately before the opportunity is lost. Once you have grabbed a picture you can then look for alternative angles

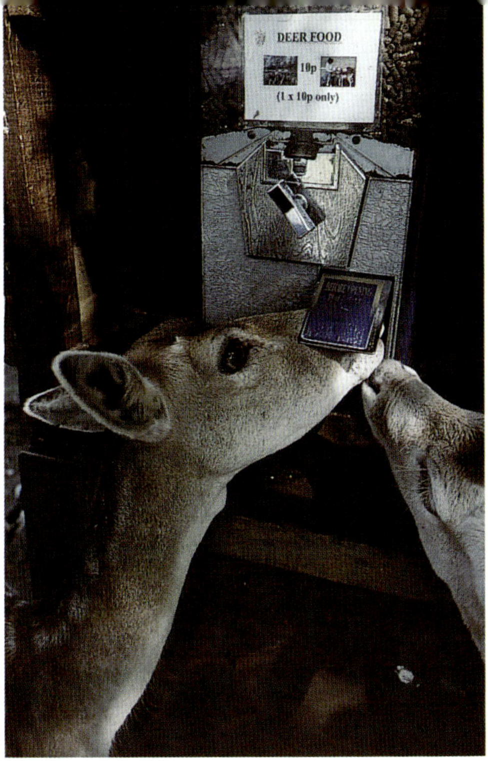

Seasonal images are valuable assets in your picture files because they are ready to help you meet publication dates at any time of the year. A dull winter's day came to life when a weak sun broke through. Sunlight will always give the necessary sparkle and texture that a snow scene requires

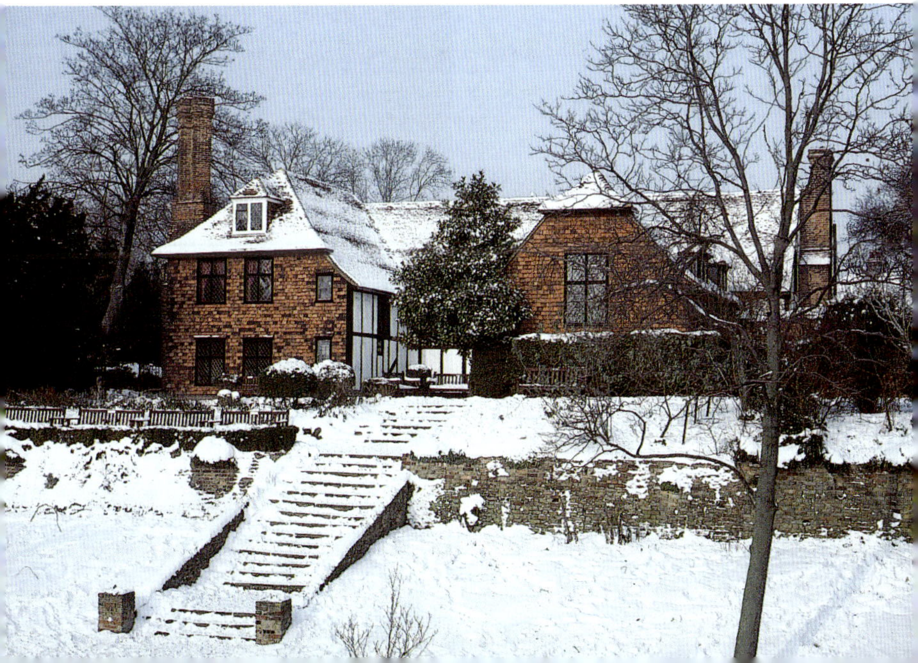

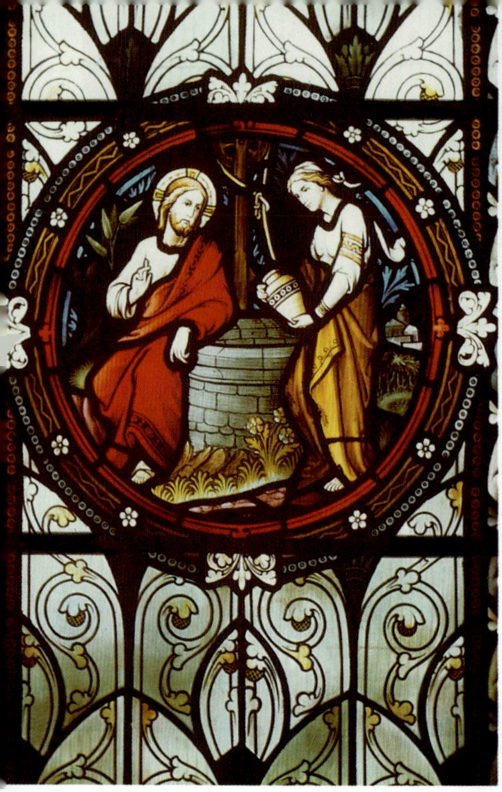

Including a photograph of a stained glass window among a set of pictures, perhaps illustrating a feature on churches, will add impact and interest to your submission. In particular, stained glass windows which portray a story can be extremely effective. If you plan to use a tripod in a cathedral or church first ask if it is permitted

The effect of the warm glow of an evening sun and a backdrop of a stormy sky existed for only a few minutes on a ferry crossing the English Channel. Obtaining the correct exposure can be troublesome in these circumstances, especially with transparency film. I had just enough time to take additional shots and bracket the exposure

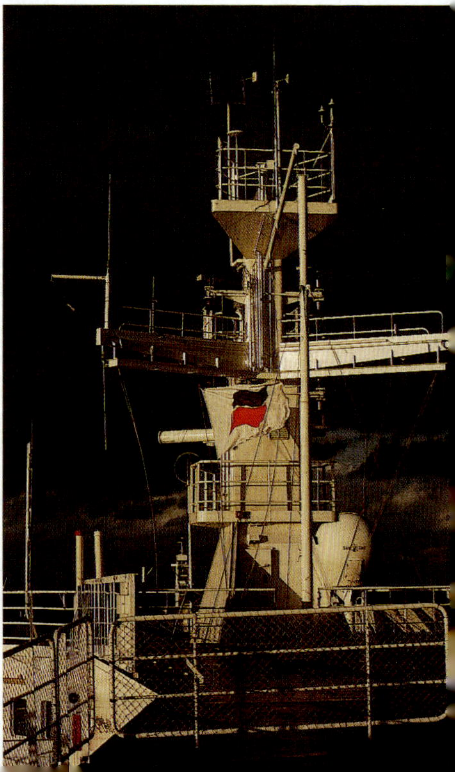

Although there is no taboo on photographs displaying converging verticals, buildings with parallel lines are usually preferable.

Alternatively, you can move farther from the subject and position the building in the top half of the frame. This, of course, will result in a greatly increased foreground, but provided the interest is subsidiary to the main subject, such as an ornamental garden or driveway, a balanced composition can be achieved and a print made from the whole negative. But if the foreground detracts from the architecture it should be cropped from the picture.

Depending on the degree of adjustment required, converging verticals can also be corrected in the darkroom at the enlarging stage. The frame which holds the paper on the enlarger baseboard can be tilted at the base of the image and the negative carrier tilted in the opposite direction to focus the picture.

Another approach to photographing high buildings is not to attempt to avoid converging verticals, but to exaggerate the effect instead. Contemporary architecture especially lends itself to this sort of treatment.

If the location is a confined area and the juxtaposition of other buildings prevents you from getting the photographs you seek, consider obtaining permission to take pictures from an upper floor of another building. If that is not possible, turn your camera on part of the structure instead. Focus on entrances, archways and other distinctive architectural features.

Extra Special Subjects

Never be content with a particular viewpoint until you have checked alternative angles. When you move in close, make certain that arches, doors and windows are not cut off at the edge of the photograph. For subjects which are particularly important to your writing it is worth visiting a location at different times of the day – even perhaps in different seasons if there are trees in the scene and you are on a long-term assignment – to ensure the best possible conditions for the job.

Stained-glass Windows

Stained-glass windows also make striking pictures, but achieving the correct exposure is not always straightforward when photographing them from the inside of a church. It is important to bear in mind that they are illuminated by light passing through the glass, and that conditions outside will affect the exposure.

Because of the variety of colours and different densities of glass, ensure that any exposure reading is taken from a mid-tone colour. As a safety factor, use the method of bracketing your exposures and take extra shots at one stop above and below the setting indicated by the meter.

Photographing Animals

Be Alert to Every Opportunity

You should never pass up opportunities to photograph animals. Even if your immediate plans do not include them, well-composed photographs of domestic pets or wildlife are popular, and it will do no harm to expand your picture files. Maybe your results will provide some ideas for articles too.

Patience is the name of the game, whether you are taking photos of a mischievous puppy in the lounge or a monkey at the zoo. But, as you bide your time to catch a fleeting pose, be prepared for the unpredictable and ready to capture an impromptu antic which may result in a photograph far more striking than the most painstaking picture arrangement.

Domestic Pets

If you have photogenic pets of your own, you will have the benefit of knowing their characteristics and habits. As a general rule, photographing animals indoors helps to restrict them to specific areas, which is especially useful when working with kittens or puppies. They are delightful subjects, but they seldom remain in the same pose long enough for more than one shot. It will also help you to maintain control of a photo session if you keep the pets occupied. Although it is preferable not to have onlookers in the room, an assistant will leave you free to concentrate on composing the image in the viewfinder. Neither you nor your helper should show annoyance when an animal does not react as planned: gentle persuasion is always kinder and more effective.

A well-thought-out viewpoint is vital in emphasizing the appeal of domestic animals. Standing at full height with the camera pointing towards the floor will invariably diminish the pet's appearance and detract from the natural charm of the picture. Placing a kitten or a puppy on a table or armchair covered with a blanket gives you a better chance of taking pictures at their level and allows you to operate from a comfortable working height.

Delegate to your assistant the responsibility for helping with the pose and preventing the pet from straying to the edge of the table. A hot-water bottle placed under a blanket will encourage most pets to remain still for a few minutes. While the pet enjoys the warmth your assistant should stand near you and attract its attention.

Ensure that you have a selection of props handy. Anything from a ball of wool to a cardboard box can make a cat playful or become absorbed in stalking. For a puppy an old slipper can be used to good effect and will usually achieve a cute response.

It is not advisable to offer food as an incentive in a confined area – it usually encourages the animal to move towards the dish rather than turn its head, and the pose is lost. However, a dab of butter or honey on a dog's nose will help you to achieve worthwhile shots as the titbit is licked enthusiastically. Similarly, cats find fish paste irresistible, and just a little on a paw or the nose can set you up for a series of appealing pictures.

The comfort of a hot-water bottle and licking favourite flavours can induce sleepiness in the liveliest of pets. Unless they remain wide-eyed it is wise to adjourn the session to another day; a weary pet is the last thing you want. The golden rule for this type of photography is that the animal's eyes must appear alert and in sharp focus.

When taking animal pictures indoors, a flash will help to arrest movement, but if the flashgun is close to the camera lens a form of 'red eye' can occur. With a cat or a dog an annoying blue-green glow in the eyes can be caused. With an SLR camera, as we have seen, you can overcome the problem with bounce flash or by using an extension lead to hold the flashgun farther away from the lens. Some compact cameras have a pre-flash system to reduce the unwanted glow in eyes. If you are unable to use either of these suggestions and are using a flash on the camera, encourage the animal to look slightly away from the lens. It will usually help to reduce the problem. (However, this method does not seem to work so successfully with people.)

Although a standard lens will suffice for the situations we have considered so far, for smaller pets such as caged birds, guinea pigs and hamsters there are other techniques which will help to fill the frame. If you have a macro, telephoto or zoom lens you should have no trouble in getting closer to the subject. Close focusing can also be achieved with supplementary close-up lenses. They are available in various degrees of magnification and screw into the filter thread on the front of a standard lens. With any lens that gives a short camera-to-subject distance, flash shots might require very small f-stops. Also, an animal could be upset by flash at close range. Bounce flash is a useful alternative on such occasions.

Photographing pets outdoors means faster shutter speeds and the benefit of sunlight accentuating the texture of fur and feathers. But instead of following a cat, dog or rabbit around the garden, focus on a predetermined zone and then cajole the animal into that area, using similar methods of enticement to those suggested for indoor photography. A length of string and a ball are also useful. Try shooting from low viewpoints, but do not forget to check the background before firing the shutter.

Down on the Farm

Whereas domestic pets can be manoeuvred into a good pose and encouraged to perform, farm animals necessitate a different approach. It is important to have more than one theme in mind and to try a series of shots. In addition to pastoral scenes of cattle or horses grazing, take pictures of animals in the farmyard as well.

If you live near a farm or you are planning a holiday in the vicinity of one, contact the farmer and ask for permission to take some pictures. If your request is granted, discover the workaday happenings, the feeding and milking times. Consider using farm machinery or buildings as backdrops, as they will contribute to the atmosphere.

Zoos and Safari Parks

Zoos house a wide variety of animals, and if the occupants of one enclosure are not in a satisfactory position for photographing you can easily move on to another. There will be more opportunities for pictures before or during feeding times, but it is a good idea to observe an animal for a while before taking a picture to establish its behaviour and walking patterns, making it easier to anticipate movements and the right moment to press the shutter release.

One problem you are likely to encounter is a large compound in which the animals are too far away to get an image of reasonable size. Unless you have a telephoto lens, do not waste your film. Wire netting is another unsatisfactory intrusion in animal photographs, but it can be eliminated by using a wide aperture and holding your camera close to the wire. Take care not to go too close, however, and put yourself or your equipment at risk.

In small zoos it is sometimes difficult to find natural backgrounds. This is not such an issue in safari parks, but you do have to stay in your car, which means you will miss out on the choice of alternative viewpoints. Before entering the park make sure the car windows are clean, because once you are inside safety regulations demand that all windows remain closed. If possible, let someone else do the driving so that you can give all your attention to photography.

Not all the animals will be close to the car tracks, but even those farther away can provide a good picture if the surroundings are attractive. Monkeys are usually among the adventurous types and will offer plenty of photo opportunities around or on the vehicle.

A standard lens should be adequate for a wide range of shots in a safari park, although something like a 75–150 mm or 70–210 mm zoom lens would give you the advantage of precise framing. Whatever camera you use, keep the lens close to the car window to prevent reflections, choose a fast shutter speed to eliminate movement, and take plenty of film.

Birds

For those who wish to take pictures of wildlife in its natural environment, bird photography is a good place to start. Nature reserves have permanent hides which have been erected in places where wildlife is most likely to be seen. These allow the photographer to remain concealed in relative comfort.

Birds in towns and parks are used to having people around and are usually prepared to come reasonably close. They are also readily attracted by food. If you have a garden, you can tempt a number of species by hanging a mesh bag of nuts from a bush, fence or tree.

Once birds are accustomed to the source of their food, you can lure them to a bird table or a branch on which you wish to focus. A camera loaded with fast film, a telephoto lens and a tripod are ideal for the task. Even if you and the equipment are hidden in the garden, the birds will scatter when they first hear the noise of the shutter, but they will gradually accept the sound and eventually ignore it.

Taking pictures from the house through an open window will cause less distraction for the birds and allow you to be more comfortable between shots. Birds near a nest are relatively easier to approach, but no picture is worth distressing the birds or causing them to abandon their nests for. The welfare of wildlife should come first in all forms of photography.

A 50 mm lens or a mid-range zoom such as 28–80 mm or 35–70 mm can be used for photographing tamer birds, which appear at ease among humans. Pigeons and seagulls present excellent picture possibilities. Shots of seagulls swooping for a piece of bread held in the hand or thrown in the air can result in worthwhile photographs. A companion who can toss the bread with accuracy into the area on which you have focused your lens is a real asset when you are attempting this type of action shot.

Photography for All Seasons

In addition to the challenge of taking pictures all the year round, it is profitable for the writer-photographer to record scenes which symbolize the four seasons. Although the themes you write about most will influence the kind of photographs you take, it is good to be aware of techniques which will help you capture the distinctive aspects of each season. For magazine use, remember that seasonal pictures are often shot for publication the following year.

Spring

Whereas summer and autumn days can be hazy, the clear visibility of spring is excellent for shooting distant detail. Spring is also a period of the year when the sun is comparatively low in the sky, giving angled lighting most of the day. This is just right for the majority of photographic projects.

In the spring, pictures of blossom, chicks, crocuses, daffodils and lambs are popular with magazines and newspapers, so if you have an opportunity to photograph these subjects, do not pass them by or assume they are commonplace. Try a fresh approach. An imaginative or unusual presentation will give your pictures the necessary extra appeal.

To emphasize the detail of blossom, get as close as your lens will permit. Whether you use black and white or colour film, clear blue sky is an ideal backdrop, but resist the temptation to put your camera away if the sky is not right. Take a few shots to record the best pictures that are possible and try again when the sky has improved. And always bear in mind that blossom can be blown away overnight.

When a flowering tree is the principal subject, ensure that it is in sharp focus. Movement of the camera and careless focusing can make the most glorious blossom look like cotton wool. The slightest breeze will also cause a fuzzy image, so ensure that you use a fast shutter speed.

Lambs gambolling in a meadow are irresistible, and a zoom or telephoto lens will be invaluable for filling the frame without getting too close to the action. Be patient – if you move too quickly, the lambs will be frightened away and you will have to wait until they have settled before starting a stealthy approach once again.

Do not overlook the potential for springtime photography in a garden. Make a daily progress check on flowers, shrubs and trees so that they can be photographed in near perfect condition. Spring weather usually includes some exceptional cloud formations which will be a bonus to scenic pictures.

Disappointing landscape photographs are often the result of cramming too much into the picture. We tend to be impressed by a vast expanse of scenery because of the far-off detail. But when the panorama is reproduced in a photograph the distant view becomes insignificant and does not appear as our eyes perceived it. This sort of problem can be avoided either by including some foreground interest or, better still, concentrating on a smaller area. Whenever you are photographing a landscape it is vital that your viewpoint is close enough to emphasize the important elements in the frame.

Summer

Summer is the time when flower beds and borders are at their best. Give careful consideration to the angle of the light. Avoid photography at midday and make the most of early-morning or late-afternoon light when the sun is lower in the sky. Remember that sidelighting will emphasize shape and texture.

Try different viewpoints to discover the most pleasing composition. If you visit one of the many gardens open to the public, take some shots from an elevated position such as a raised walkway. On an overcast day the soft lighting will cast no shadows and will reveal delicate gradation and subtle colour which is sometimes missing in photographs of flowers taken in sunlight.

Including a lake or pond in which a building or statue is reflected can give additional interest to otherwise static subject matter. One benefit of the long days of summer is that you have more time to choose the most appropriate lighting. If the water is calm, a clear mirror-like reflection can be captured. A gentle breeze blowing across the water will distort the reflected image and can be equally impressive.

Activities at the seaside or near the coast are familiar

summer scenes, with yachts and windsurfers making exciting images. The secret is to be selective and include only a few participants in the frame. If you require a picture of all the craft at the start of a yacht race, remember to avoid cutting the picture in half. Position the horizon well away from the middle of the frame.

Although rain is not confined to the summer, this is a time of the year when it can be effectively depicted, especially when showers are interspersed with bright skies. Rain can transform drab surroundings as surfaces and objects take on a magical sheen. When the rain stops the light usually gets brighter; this is a good time for taking pictures, particularly if the sun shines.

To record rain, try shutter speeds of 1/60 or 1/125 second, as this will show rain as a blur. Sidelighting and a dark shadowy background will accentuate the effect. If you photograph a landscape while it is raining, distant detail will be diffused. Another way to show rain is to photograph a scene or person through a rain-spattered windowpane and focus precisely on the wet glass.

Autumn

During autumn, the days shorten, shadows lengthen and the sun is closer to the horizon. The spectacular displays of gold and brown leaves require colour film to do them justice. Take time in choosing a viewpoint and assess the array of colour with half-closed eyes. This will help you to compose shapes and tints in a pleasing arrangement.

Refrain from taking shots of trees all from the same angle. Backlighting can produce outstanding results, so attempt to capture the sun illuminating translucent leaves and move in close to photograph individual branches.

Even though russet hues are ideal for colour reproduction, bear in mind that some publications still use black and white illustrations. With good directional lighting, leafy lanes and trees that are almost bare of leaves are strong subjects for black and white film.

If you want human interest for your autumnal shots, children throwing leaves in the air can make appealing pictures. Keep the youngsters from getting too close to each other, use a fast shutter speed and frame the action with plenty of space in the top third of your viewfinder to include the scattering leaves. Catching the expressions of children preoccupied in a game of conkers is another seasonal idea worth exploring.

Hay bales can make a striking countryside picture provided there is a sense of design in the composition. The large cylindrical-shaped bales are usually spaced about the field in an irregular way. It is advisable to concentrate on one or two as a focal point of the photograph.

Sunset shots are often spoiled by overexposure because the meter reading is taken from foreground details instead of the sky. Getting the exposure right is not always straightforward, but a reliable method for sunsets is to take a reading from an area of the sky adjacent to the sun. Whenever a sunset is extra special and you are not sure about the exposure, take additional shots at one stop above and below the indicated reading.

Dramatic photographs can be achieved by eliminating the sun itself from the picture area and emphasizing the glow caused by it setting instead. A lens hood will help to shield the lens from the effects of flare. Even when you are photographing a sunset, remember the advice that you should never look at the sun directly or, especially, through a viewfinder.

Winter

The first snowfall of winter often encourages people to bring their cameras out of hibernation. Even the most mundane view becomes captivating when covered with a carpet of snow. Yet, frequently, pictures are disappointing because they lack foreground interest. The inclusion of a fence or tree can make all the difference.

Snow has a smoothing effect on paths and grass, offering suitable settings for pictures of children making a snowman or just romping in the snow. Always take care to keep your camera out of the line of fire if snowballs are being thrown. It is also wise to protect your lens with a UV or skylight filter in addition to a lens hood. Neither filter will affect the exposure but the lens will be kept free from moisture.

Under grey cloud a snowy landscape tends to look flat and uninteresting, but sunshine reveals texture and imparts the sparkle that a snow picture requires. But even in sunlight snow can appear grey and muddy-looking in a photograph because of underexposure.

Exposure metering systems are calculated to give an average reading off an average subject, but snow is one of the brightest reflectors around. To compensate for the extra brilliance additional exposure is needed. For an average snow scene it is worth increasing exposure by one or two stops more than indicated.

When photographing people in the snow take an exposure reading from their faces, but be careful to shield your meter from the sun, otherwise it will influence the reading. If your camera does not have a built-in meter facility, refer to the exposure recommendations which accompany the film.

Hoar frost is equally photogenic, but can disappear rapidly on sunny days, so it is necessary to be up early and make for subjects such as holly, leaves and seed-heads which will be covered in a coating of ice crystals. Batteries become sluggish in cold weather and sometimes give up when you least expect it, so if your camera is battery dependent, take some spares with you.

4

Planning Photographic Projects

Illustrating an Article About an All-day Event

Before undertaking any photographic project, be sure that all your ideas for pictures have been well thought out. Leave nothing to chance. Include in your preparation a thorough check of all equipment, including batteries, and confirm that everything is in good working order.

Let us consider a situation in which an editor has replied favourably to your suggestion of an illustrated article about fairs and festivals. Having already familiarized yourself with the magazine, you will have noted the style, the number of words required and how many pictures are generally used with each feature. It is preferable to submit a selection of photographs and give the editor a choice, so aim to send two or three prints more than would normally be published with an article. Offer a variety of vertically and horizontally framed shots, giving the layout artist greater freedom in designing the pages.

Never include a print that is not relevant to the theme just to make up the number. Each picture accompanying an article should be there for a reason, but take care not to refer specifically to a photograph in the text in case it is not used.

Practical Approach

Careful planning and a practical approach will help to make the most of your opportunities for photography. Based on your article outline, decide on the pictures you require and what you want the shots to achieve. Make a list of your picture ideas so that when you attend the event you will know exactly what will enhance the text.

For large fairs and festivals it is worthwhile contacting the organizers prior to the event to explain your interest and request an official pass. This can often make photography easier by admitting you to areas not accessible to spectators. Whether you obtain special privileges or not, ensure that you arrive early on the day, obtain a programme and make a note of all the special displays. They are usually held in an enclosure, so assess the area and decide on the best positions for photography, bearing in mind the direction of the sun, which may be ideal lighting in the morning but necessitate an alternative viewpoint in the afternoon.

Try to catch the spontaneous reactions of people as they respond and relate to each other. Punch and Judy shows, which children find so absorbing, should never be disregarded. This captivating sideshow invariably generates wonderful expressions and uninhibited involvement from the youngsters.

One of the advantages of events like fairs and festivals is that, with so much going on, appealing pictures are there for the taking. Large festivals sometimes feature the arrival of a free-fall parachute team or a hot-air balloon display. With this type of demonstration, a few shots at ground level after the participants have landed may capture an unusual behind-the-scenes picture which will add a touch of originality to your selection of photographs.

Between the main displays, search out the subjects that can be found among the stalls and sideshows. This is when a wide-angle lens is useful for producing results which give an impression of the photographer being right amongst the activity. A zoom lens can provide additional versatility, enabling you to attempt shots which otherwise might not be possible.

However, it would be wrong to suggest that a choice of lenses is a prerequisite for pictures of people enjoying themselves. Either a 35 mm SLR with a 50 mm lens (or a mid-range zoom of, say 35–70 mm) or a compact camera will cope remarkably well, but, in the excitement, do not forget to fill the frame.

Films for the Job

For colour photographs film with a speed rating of ISO 100 is adequate on a bright day, but for cloudy, dull conditions a faster film speed of ISO 200 or 400 is preferable. If your camera is to be loaded with black and white film, ISO 100 or 125 should cover most situations. Keep ISO 400 for poor light. Do not forget XP2, the chromogenic ISO 400 film and its fine grain, which makes it an all-rounder.

Craft or floral displays are usually exhibited in a marquee, so you have a choice of using flash or making the most of the canvas-diffused light, which gives shadowless and fairly even illumination. Photography under canvas, without flash and on a dull day, calls for a slow shutter speed and a camera support, but using a tripod in a crowded tent is not only hazardous to other people, it puts your camera at risk as well. This is the sort of situation where a special pass will enable you to take pictures before the marquee is opened to the public.

Apart from decorated stalls, keep your eyes open for candid pictures as you move among the crowds. This kind of photograph will inject a 'slice of life' into a set of illustrations with a fairs and festivals theme, but you need to press the shutter release the instant you see a likely subject, before the chance disappears.

Pre-focusing

On such occasions you will barely have time to focus. This is when an auto-focus system can prove its worth. But even if you have to focus manually all is not lost, because you can employ the technique of pre-focusing. Simply focus the lens at about 12 ft and ensure that you keep that distance from any likely subject.

To make getting candid shots even simpler, load a fast (ISO 400 speed) film and set the lens to a medium or small f-stop, i.e. between f8 and f22. This maintains a good depth of field with all but telephoto lenses, and allows for some error in judging distance. You can then concentrate on the moment to fire the shutter without having to make focusing adjustments.

Making Backgrounds Work for You

Backgrounds can be troublesome, especially when performers are surrounded by spectators. Keeping the crowds out of focus is one way of isolating a subject. Use either a medium to wide f-stop or a telephoto (or 'long' zoom) lens. Remember, a relatively wide aperture creates a shallow zone of focus, and the magnification of a long lens tends to do the same.

An alternative approach is to include onlookers, concentrating on those taking part. Try using backgrounds to your advantage by positioning yourself to take bright subjects against dark areas; for example, you could emphasize the flames of a fire-eater's act against the dark foliage of trees.

Tug-of-war contests contain all the necessary ingredients for dramatic photographs, with the benefit that the action occurs within a predictable area, ideal for pre-focusing. A shot of a few contestants taking the strain is often more striking than a picture of the entire team. A zoom lens can be invaluable, enabling you to fill the frame with several sections of the action without moving from your position. If you do not possess a zoom, get as close as possible to ensure a reasonably sized image in the viewfinder. One of the best moments to capture the tense encounter is when the teams match each other in effort and the rope becomes almost motionless. This is when the contestants' positions, as well as their facial expressions, change very slowly.

Centuries ago, people would gather from miles around to watch jousting contests and swordplay. These days mock battles are proving just as popular. The devotees who re-enact the engagements wear uniform and armour, authentic in almost every detail, and skilfully wield their weapons in exhilarating combat. One of these displays alone could be the source of all the pictures required for several illustrated articles.

Make sure that you check the camera settings before the start. Once the 'battle' commences, action is fast and dramatic with little time for a second glance. A large number of warriors can be skirmishing at the same time, so for the sake of variety do not keep your camera aimed only at one group. Again, a zoom lens will help you to fill the frame precisely.

Panning Technique

If you are photographing vehicles such as go-karts, an impression of speed can be conveyed by panning the camera. It is a technique which keeps the vehicle sharp and the background blurred. The best results are obtained when a moving subject passes across the angle of view.

The first attempts at panning can be disappointing, but if you tackle the technique in stages you will be more likely to succeed. If your camera has to be focused manually, focus on the area where you anticipate the vehicle will be when you fire the shutter. Keep relaxed and point the lens towards the approaching vehicle.

The second stage is to keep the vehicle in the same position in the viewfinder as you follow its course with a smooth sweep of the camera, releasing the shutter when it reaches the place on which you originally focused. Remember to continue the sweeping movement until after the shutter has closed to avoid any jerking of the camera during the exposure.

The result should be a sharp image of the vehicle against a blurred background, which will give an impression of speed. If you can control the shutter speed, start with a setting of 1/60 second and make notes for future reference. A shutter speed that is too fast will 'freeze' the vehicle's wheels and make it appear stationary.

The above suggestions do not cover the full range, but they are an indication of the diversity of picture situations that can arise at fairs and festivals. Try to capture as many different subjects as possible to provide a reasonable balance of action and human interest in your final choice of pictures.

If you need to reload your camera with film on a sunny

day, find a shady spot; failing that, create shade by turning your back to the sun. It is also sensible not to use a make of film that is unfamiliar to you when you are on an assignment. If you want to experiment with a brand of film try it out on subjects that are not one-off events and can easily be reshot.

Although fairs and festivals have been used as an example here, the suggestions made above can also be applied to other events. But wherever you go, if you can sense the atmosphere or the fun of the occasion, it will be reflected in your writing and in your photography too.

Illustrating a Non-fiction Book

Planning photography for a long-term project such as a book calls for a careful assessment of possible pictures and what you seek to portray. In the early days, illustrating a book can be a daunting prospect. A structured routine is therefore necessary to maintain the theme and clarify the purpose of each picture.

When you are confident that your idea is worth submitting, prepare your proposal with care. If a publisher shows an interest, it is important to find out the picture origination requirements and the preferred number of photographs expected for the kind of book you are preparing. At this stage it will also be helpful to establish whether the illustrations are to be in colour, black and white, or both. You can then prepare the photographs in the way the publisher prefers.

If you already have a collection of photographs you could use, make sure sure the ones you choose are of the right quality. This will be especially important if, for example, the images are mainly colour photographs and it is likely that all the illustrations will be printed in black and white. In these days of advanced reproduction methods certain origination difficulties can be overcome. Excellent black and white images can be obtained from colour prints, as long as they are well produced. In a similar way colour prints can be produced from good colour transparencies. But although techniques continue to evolve, remember that book publishers usually favour transparencies, so before you undertake photography for a book project it is essential to find out a publisher's preferences, particularly where colour images are concerned.

Photographs can be a significant factor in a book. The selection of illustrations in relation to the text is as important as the order of the chapters themselves. The right blend of words and pictures is a basic requirement in persuading booksellers to put the book on their shelves. Handling the photography yourself gives you the advantage of producing images that exactly match your theme.

Whether pictures or text should be produced first depends on the type of book you are working on. With a writer who specializes in travel articles and has built up a stock of photographs over several years the writing would probably follow the illustrations. But someone producing a 'how to' book might prefer to take pictures after the text is completed.

If you already have photographs on file which relate to your chosen subject you must carefully assess each image and decide if it fits in with the theme. When you first consider writing a non-fiction book, it is usually advisable to plan your illustration strategy and start getting your pictures together as early as possible.

Do not rely on your memory to retain ideas for photographs. Prepare notes and, where appropriate, some rough sketches. File them in an accessible envelope system and draw up a chart of all photographs that are required. Just as a book is planned in outline and chapters, plan your pictures in a similar way so that the photographs slot into place in the overall structure of the project.

By working to your picture script and taking pictures from more than one viewpoint – in both close-up and long-shot – you will be able to cover your subject from several angles. This will provide a range of alternative images at editing time and raise the standard in the final selection of pictures, without complicating the process of selection.

When examining your photographs always consider whether they help fulfil your original purpose. Also ask yourself if each picture has the appeal or impact to maintain interest and keep readers absorbed in the theme. In addition to scrutinizing each shot individually, spread all the pictures out for an overview. This will show you not only which make most impact, but also which are below standard. The latter should be re-taken. If this is impracticable, withdraw the poor pictures from your selection anyway. It is preferable to submit fewer pictures rather than weaken the overall appearance with poor shots. All of which reinforces the fact that you should not be miserly with film, especially on a long-term project such as illustrating a book.

When pictures and words are eventually brought together, appraise the outcome as a complete package and assess the overall effect on the basis of your initial concept. Even at this late stage consider if improvements could be made by replacing any of the photographs.

Unless you have had previous experience, it is advisable to

avoid borrowing photographs yourself from picture libraries or agencies. If you consider certain pictures are important to your text, it is preferable to let your publisher make the necessary arrangements. It is also worthwhile enquiring if the publisher is willing to include the cost of borrowing pictures in the project's budget.

Travel Photography

Earlier in this chapter I stressed that a disciplined approach is necessary to achieve publishable pictures for a feature about an all-day event. Similar planning is also important for coverage spanning a longer period, particularly if the objects or places you are photographing are not in your locality, as in travel photography.

Illustrations are almost invariably needed to accompany travel writing and illustrating your features with your own photographs brings life to the text and is an enjoyable complement to your writing. So let us consider how you can increase the chances of taking good travel pictures.

Successful travel photography entails more than simply taking pictures of famous monuments and celebrated tourist attractions. Although architecture and ancient stones are important elements in the travel scene, it is the 'everyday life' shots which can inject realism into a set of travel pictures.

To capture inspiring travel pictures, as I have said, requires diligent preparation. Before setting off, therefore, discover all you can about your destination from guidebooks, maps, brochures and by visiting your public library. Illustrated books will give you information about specific locations, climate and culture. If necessary, call on travel agents and contact tourist boards for further details.

With photography as well as your writing in mind, carry out a market study of the publications which feature travel and could be likely targets for your work. Jot down your findings together with possible topics and the approach you intend to take. Also prepare a list of photographs which you consider will be essential.

Before departure check that your equipment insurance cover is adequate. If your camera looks new, get a photocopy of the purchase receipt, which you may need for customs purposes. Also prepare a list of all your equipment, including serial numbers. Make several copies and leave one at home. The details could come in useful at the customs counter or if you are unfortunate enough to have anything stolen.

Film and X-ray Machines

When travelling by air, do not pack your films in a suitcase or bag that will travel in the hold as the X-ray machines used to check any suspect baggage in the hold are likely to be more powerful than those used for hand luggage. The best precaution is to carry your photographic equipment in a camera bag or holdall as hand luggage.

Despite the assurances by airport authorities that security X-ray machines are harmless to film, photographers continue to remain suspicious. Most airports claim that machines will not fog film rated below ISO 1000. However, X-rays can have a cumulative effect, so if you are travelling to several places by air and your films have to pass through a number of machines, beware!

Asking for your films to be hand checked will not win you any popularity votes, but airport staff may accede to a polite request. If you put all your films in a clear plastic bag it will make checking easier. Let the remainder of your photographic gear go through the X-ray machine to keep the security staff happy, and repack the film in your camera bag before leaving the airport.

I have never encountered problems with this method although on one occasion when I requested a hand search of my camera bag, the official insisted that camera backs should be opened for inspection. No harm was done, but a loaded camera could mean lost pictures. Be warned: in some countries photography is forbidden at airports, and remember not to point your lens at military installations and personnel.

Capturing the Mood on Film

Upon arriving at your destination, track down the tourist information office and enquire about carnivals or other festivities. A friendly hotel receptionist can also be invaluable for giving advice on bus services, markets and the prevailing attitude towards photographers. But do not let your photography be overcome by the excitement of your new surroundings. Just as you regularly make notes which will be the ingredients for travel articles, always keep in mind your plan for photographs, while remaining alert for unplanned pictures.

Capturing the mood of a place is not easy. Personal impressions can be influenced by many things, whereas it is only your visual perception which is conveyed on film. Some photographers try to sum up a place in one photograph. When they manage to do so the result can be outstanding, but it usually takes a number of attempts to achieve it, so never merely hope for the best and limit yourself to just one shot of a subject.

When you are attracted by a scene, strive to capture the splendour which first caught your eye. Try to translate what is before you into a compelling picture through your choice of viewpoint and strong composition. Even if you cannot fulfil your original intention, it is important to record the scene on film – you may not get a second chance.

People in Their Environment

Photographs showing people in their environment are essential in any sequence of travel shots. Yet this often causes the most problems for photographers. Not everyone likes to be photographed; there may be cultural, religious or superstitious objections. Some people may also only agree if they receive monetary reward. Paying for the privilege of getting this kind of shot is rarely satisfactory; results frequently lack spontaneity and can appear badly posed. Some photographers who use a Polaroid camera find that giving the person an instant print is preferable to handing over money.

Normally if people are approached in a friendly manner, language and posing problems can be overcome. Provided you do not rush them, most people are happy about having their photograph taken; country folk are especially willing to pose. Craftsmen and souvenir sellers are generally co-operative whether they make a sale or not – usually a friendly acknowledgement is all that is required. However, these colourful characters often provide a number of pictures, so you might show your appreciation by buying something from them. And no matter how willing people may appear to be, do not overstay your welcome.

If you are hesitant about photographing strangers abroad, you can gain confidence by attending some of the events which are especially put on for tourists. Moreover, your pre-journey research may have found out about local festivals. At such times photography is expected, so you can use your camera without embarrassment.

Markets

Markets have universal appeal. Whether they deal in fruit, spices or camels, be prepared to make the most of every opportunity for a picture. If you do not have an auto-focus lens, use the same technique as suggested for candid pictures earlier in this chapter. Pre-focus a standard 50 mm lens at about 12 ft or a 28 mm wide-angle lens at about 9 ft. Keep to those distances when photographing activity around the stalls and displays with your camera set at a medium or small f-stop, from f8 to f22.

If you are using a telephoto lens in a crowded area, an elevated viewpoint is preferable. This avoids the problem of people passing to and fro between your lens and the subject. With a telephoto lens, you will probably have the advantage that the person in your viewfinder is unaware of the camera, but his or her face will be isolated against an out-of-focus background. However, this will reveal nothing of the surroundings, which may be ideal for a portrait but unsuitable for relating the subject to the environment. Another tip worth remembering in markets is that the broad view of a wide-angle lens is useful for including people off-centre in a picture without them having any idea they are in the frame.

Buildings

A sightseeing bus tour is invaluable for discovering buildings and places which are suitable for a photographic exploration. The inclusion of architecture in a sequence of travel pictures always generates interest. Internationally famous landmarks such as the Eiffel Tower, the Statue of Liberty or the Taj Mahal are often used to set the scene. Apart from being immediately recognizable, a traditional view of a well-known building may not do anything else for a travel feature, but a shot from an unusual angle, or a picture taken early or late in the day – perhaps an illuminated shot after dark – can provide impact. If you prefer not to carry the additional weight of a tripod on the off-chance that a night shot will present itself, try to find a low wall or a box on which to support your hands and camera while making a time exposure.

When shooting travel pictures, take note of visual clues that will make the picture look dated in the future, such as a famous building under renovation, current fashions and cars.

The Reassurance of a Back-up Camera

Having a second camera in your equipment bag is reassuring when travelling overseas. The nightmare which can be caused by a faulty camera can be averted if you have another model as the back-up. So think about buying a spare camera, either new or second-hand. If you own a compact camera with a standard lens and are satisfied with its performance, by all means buy another compact as a back-up, but try to get one that will give you additional versatility, such as a compact with a 35–105 mm zoom lens. If you have a 35 mm SLR, consider purchasing a second body of the same make (or type – for certain makes of camera share the same basic design of lens mount); lenses will fit either body. Seek out a second-hand bargain; shopping around could result in a deal which includes a telephoto or zoom lens – again increasing your scope.

If you do buy a camera for a trip abroad, try it out with a roll of film on a range of different subjects and check the results before going away. As always, take more film than you think you will need; there is nothing worse than trying to find a store with a fresh stock of your favourite film. Also take a supply of spare batteries.

Travel Pictures Nearer Home

Travel photography suggests faraway places. It can also involve taking pictures nearer home. But good planning is still essential. Learning about an area through careful research is an important part of your preparation. The internet can also be a valuable information resource.

If you were journeying through Yorkshire making notes and taking photographs for a fresh angle on the Brontë family, for example, your picture list would obviously include the village of Haworth, and photographs of the parish church, the parsonage, the cobbled main street, the gift shop which was once the druggist's store that Branwell patronized, and the moors, would all be essential. But in addition to taking shots from more than one viewpoint, the bustling village activity might also prompt further picture ideas.

The photographs which result from an assignment such as the foregoing should blend as a picture essay. Taking a sequence of photographs in this way will help to improve your skills in interpreting the theme of an article visually.

On some occasions you might revisit familiar places which you have photographed before. When this occurs try to improve on your previous pictures and attempt to inject extra impact and appeal. Do not forget to take some shots of inscriptions and plaques which can be so useful when you are collating information about a location.

5
Effective Presentation

Catching the Editor's Eye

Competent presentation is likely to catch the editor's eye and encourage interest in your contribution, although it will never disguise poor photography. When you submit photographs to accompany an article they should be presented and packaged in a professional manner. A fundamental of good presentation is that your work should always conform to the picture requirements of the magazine you are targeting.

Some publications request colour illustrations only, some specify just black and white, whereas others use both. As I explained in chapter 1, magazines that are printed in colour generally prefer to receive transparencies as origination for colour reproduction. However, most will consider good quality colour prints if excessive enlargement is not needed. All prints for reproduction should be on glossy, not matt paper.

Although black and white illustrations can be produced from colour prints, it is still better to submit black and white prints when they are requested. Even if you are acquainted with the latest reproduction techniques, always find out exactly in what form an editor requires illustrations to be supplied. Whatever kind of origination you submit, it is imperative that the processing is beyond reproach.

Importance of Quality Processing

Good processing is an integral part of eye-catching presentation. Bearing in mind that the majority of photographic processors are geared for colour photography, you will need to know of an efficient and reliable service which can also take care of your black and white developing and printing.

If you want to assess your photographs without delay, colour processing can be obtained quickly. High street mini-labs offer a one-hour service, and others can also arrange a quick turn-round service. However, black and white processing is not that fast, although smooth presentation sometimes depends on getting black and white photographs produced quickly too.

Developing black and white films yourself has its advantages, in these cases. You can then evaluate the images within a few hours of photographing the subject. It would also overcome the difficulties that are sometimes experienced in finding a local service specializing in processing black and white films.

When taking black and white pictures, you should seriously consider having a 10 in × 8 in contact sheet made from each film as an alternative to ordering prints when the film is taken in for developing. All the frames of a film can be compared and scrutinized through a magnifying glass before selecting the images for enlargement. Contact prints are also ideal for filing purposes and keeping records.

Even when a scene has been carefully composed in the

camera's viewfinder, there are occasions when an improvement can be made by cropping some of the image at the enlarging stage. The proportions of the 35 mm frame, for instance, do not suit all subjects, so a selective enlargement can be made. Instructions to the processor should not be passed on verbally, but prominently indicated on the contact print with an all-surface pen or a blue chinagraph pencil.

Chromogenic Film

Apart from taking the pictures, you may not want to take up any more of your writing time by getting involved in black and white developing and contact printing. An alternative which facilitates rapid processing of black and white film is Ilford's XP2 Super. It is a fine-grain fast film, ISO 400, with excellent sharpness and wide exposure latitude.

It uses colour dye technology instead of the conventional silver image of black and white films and it can be processed alongside colour negative film in C-41 chemistry. This means that high-street mini-labs can offer a one-hour processing service and provide quality negatives which give monochrome results on colour paper. The prints do have a slight sepia tint, but subsequent enlargements can be made on conventional black and white paper in the normal way. The film can also be processed in Ilford XP2 Super chemistry by specialist black and white processors but you then lose the benefit of a quick turn round.

A chromogenic film such as Ilford XP2 Super is an excellent choice when you are facing a very tight deadline or if you find yourself miles from home and need to take photographs in black and white. Before leaving the district you can confirm that the images you want are safely on film by using the local mini-lab service. When abroad, towards the end of the trip you may get a professional laboratory or a reputable mini-lab to process your films 'same-day' or 'overnight'.

Improving Non-digital Camera Images on Your Computer

Digital camera owners have the benefit of being able to view their results straight away. They can subsequently download the images to a computer and enhance the pictures before printing. Even if you do not use a digital camera but like the idea of improving your photographs on a computer, you might consider purchasing a scanner to digitize images taken on a non-digital camera. The value of this is that it enables you to enhance your images at the final stages, especially those which are creatively portrayed. Flatbed scanners are available for prints (and artwork), and film scanners will accept both transparencies and negatives. Scanners also differ in resolution values, with the higher number of pixels being found in the more expensive models.

There is another way to digitize your pictures. When you hand in an unprocessed C-41 film to a participating dealer, you can order not only negatives and prints but also a Photo CD comprising a complete set of digitized images which can be viewed on your monitor and subsequently printed. You can also take along ten or more slides or negatives from your files and ask for them to be recorded on to a Photo CD. When you have the CD, pop it into a computer and work with ready-scanned images. View them, manipulate them and print them. You can also e-mail or upload them.

Print Sizes for Reproduction

Although 10 in × 8 in or 8½ in × 6½ in (whole plate) enlargements are acknowledged as acceptable sizes for reproduction, it does not mean that you must submit those sizes without deviation. For example, if you are submitting a large number of prints to a magazine on a speculative basis, the cost of materials can be an important consideration. It is worth checking the sizes of the illustrations printed in the periodical you have in your sights. If nothing larger than 7 in × 5 in is published, then prints of that size can be adequate in some circumstances. However, larger prints are usually preferred. Comparison of a smaller print with a 10 in × 8 in enlargement will demonstrate the advantages of the bigger size. Detail and quality will be more evident and the larger image will look more impressive when viewed on the desk of a busy editor.

Borderless prints are the style for both colour and black and white. Pictures with a white border are not fashionable, although they are favoured by some photographers who like to enhance monochrome prints with a neat margin. Editors do not seem to mind one way or the other. But borderless or not, never submit a print with damaged corners or edges, and be sure that the prints look fresh.

Scrutinizing Each Picture from an Editor's Viewpoint

One of the most important aspects of successful presentation is, of course, the image itself. Try to imagine yourself in a busy editorial office and assess your package of photographs objectively. Does each picture complement the text? Is there a print that appears to be there to make up the number rather than being included on merit? Were you influenced in choosing a certain image because of the difficulties you encountered at the time the shot was taken?

Your objective analysis should start when you are looking at a print for the first time since you captured the scene in the viewfinder. As you view each photograph appraise it critically. If you are dissatisfied with the result consider whether an improvement could be made by astute cropping. Ascertain if the scene could be more effectively positioned in the frame by excluding the foreground. Check if alternative shots on the same film would be more suitable. This is when a contact sheet of all the images can be a useful aid in your assessment.

First impressions are so vital when the envelope containing your manuscript and photographs is opened in an editorial office. After selecting the pictures which best illustrate your text, try to assess them overall from an editor's viewpoint. Survey them dispassionately and check for any technical shortcomings such as poor focus or general lack of sharpness. Do not risk spoiling a good presentation by including anything below standard, even if it means discarding a favourite shot.

If you get the opportunity, look at the original transparencies or prints of good illustrations in a magazine or book. Are your images as clear, as sharp and – especially in black and white – with a full range of tones? In prints notice the detail in the whole tonal scale from white to black – are your prints sparkling or 'flat'?

Marking up Instructions

Presentation is equally important when you are marking up

instructions for prints which will be reproduced in an illustrated book. If the subject requires an area to be trimmed or overprinted with type, it must be specified on an overlay. Fold a sheet of paper to cover the photograph and fix it to the reverse side of the print with adhesive tape. Details should be indicated on the overlay. The information can be added before attaching the overlay to the back of the print to avoid damaging the photograph. Reproduction and other instructions will also be marked on the reverse side, but leave that to the publisher and printer.

It is essential to give each illustration a number which should be written on the manuscript and keyed into the text where the picture will be most appropriate. A caption should be affixed to the back of the print. The printers will position the relevant picture as close as possible to the indicated position.

Retouching Prints

Consider your photographs as a pictorial supplement to your writing, so ensure that they are presented in the best possible way. Check your pictures for any defects such as dust spots, which will appear on your prints as white marks or hair lines, and are caused by dust settling on the film at the enlarging stage. The greater the degree of enlargement the more prominent the flaw becomes. Any blemishes which impair the quality of the photograph and distract from the subject matter should be concealed with a dye or spotting medium.

Glossy retouching watercolour paint can be purchased in tubes and is useful if you have no experience of spotting. Any mistakes can be wiped off the print with a damp cloth. One drawback is that when the watercolour dries out it leaves visible surface marks on glossy prints, so it is not suitable for large areas of retouching. Also available are retouching dyes which penetrate the emulsion of a photograph without leaving any residue on the surface, so that any spotting is practically invisible. A kit for treating colour prints comprises concentrated dyes in 1 oz bottles. Colours can also be purchased separately.

A basic kit for treating black and white prints contains one bottle each of neutral, blue black and olive black. The colours can be mixed and diluted to match any shade required. As with the colour kit, the dyes penetrate the surface, making the spotting imperceptible.

Both watercolour and dye should be applied with a good quality artist's brush. Size 00 is usually recommended, but it is also worth working with a larger one, such as size 2, as the spotting medium does not dry out as quickly as with smaller brushes. It is important to work with the brush almost dry, in a near vertical position, and lightly stipple the offending spot until it blends with the adjacent tone or colour. If the brush is too wet the dye will be harder to control. For larger marks, start at the edge of the defect by applying the dye with a succession of minute dots, gradually working towards the middle until the blemish matches the surrounding area. Never attempt to retouch a white line with a single stroke of the brush, but treat it with a series of dots as with a white spot.

Black marks are less common but can be more troublesome to remove. One method is to apply an intermixed bleach and accelerator solution with an artist's brush. The solution can be diluted with water, according to whether a gradual or fast bleaching action is required. It is best to work on a wet print. After the blemish is removed and the bleached area rinsed with water, a solution of hypo fixer should be applied to the treated area for 30 seconds to make the changes permanent. The print should then be washed in water for five minutes. It is important to follow the instruction leaflet very carefully. When dry, the bleached marks can be retouched where necessary with dye.

Fibre-tip Pens

There is a product called SpotPen which some people find simplifies these techniques. The pens comprise a system which disposes of the process of mixing colours. The pens are obtainable in sets of ten and each has a long-lasting nylon fibre tip similar to a size 000 artist's brush. SpotPen dyes penetrate the emulsion without leaving surface drying marks and each pen is colour coded to denote its dye. If you make an error, the dye dries sufficiently slowly for the print's surface to be wiped clean.

A useful aid for improving colour prints is a 'red eye' remover pen, which contains a transparent dye that takes away the redness in eyes caused by flash photography. The problem area is treated by retouching with a succession of dots until the red effect is eliminated. A pen which removes the glow in pets' eyes which is similarly caused by flash is also available. As with any kind of print correction, always experiment first on an unwanted photograph.

Captions

Do not overlook the importance of picture captions. They both complement and support photographs. When the prints are part of a words-and-pictures package, ensure that all the caption information is pertinent to the picture, the article and the magazine's readership. Make a point of familiarizing yourself with the style of captions that is normally used in any publication for which you are writing.

A caption also has a role to play in confirming the reader's understanding of an illustration. Although a photograph can be appreciated for its pictorial value, a caption can explain or refer to points of interest that are not so apparent. For a book, it is essential that both captions and photographs relate to and strengthen the text and that the text is relevant to the illustrations.

It is not good form to state in a caption what is obvious in an illustration. Captions should complement an image, giving information which is not evident in the shot. For example, a colour picture may show a red mountain against a blue sky. One caption might say, 'This red mountain, dramatic against the blue of the sky, is Bell Rock, several hundred feet high, near Sedona.' But a better one might be, 'Bell Rock, hundreds of feet high, is just a few miles south-east of Sedona, and sits right alongside the highway to Interstate.' Readers can see that the picture is dramatic, and they can see the colours and the mountainous character; yet they will not necessarily have the other details. Of course, the caption to a black and white picture could well include descriptions of colour.

Whether a caption provides technical information, clarifies historical details or gives the names of locations, check each line for its accuracy and verify that nothing is ambiguous or misleading. To help achieve this, keep a notebook handy in your camera bag and gather any details that will be likely caption material at the time you shoot the pictures. It may not be possible to follow up later, and in any case a caption should never appear to be an afterthought.

Writers will be familiar with the importance of employing the following six words when interviewing or researching: Who? What? Where? When? Why? How? Applying some or all these key questions to a photograph should give you the information for an appropriate caption.

When giving the details of people, ensure that the sequence of names corresponds with their positions in the photograph. You should always record the names to read from the left. Check and recheck the spelling of all names.

Some photographs will require a long caption because of the specialized nature of the description. But in all circumstances guard against captions which appear long-winded.

Captions should be typed on separate slips of paper, about one-third the size of the prints, and attached to the reverse side of the prints with a strip of clear adhesive tape. For identification purposes the slips should also bear the title of the project. Each caption and picture should be identically numbered to correspond with a complete list of illustrations and captions, which should always accompany the manuscript. Obviously, house styles vary, and another approach is to type the caption on a slip of paper that is nearly full print width, which is attached by adhesive tape to the back-lower edge of the print. Or you could put the number on the back of the print using a soft pencil and type a complete set of captions, on A4 paper, for all the illustrations, quoting the reference numbers.

You should also fix a label bearing your name, address and a copyright symbol, in a lower corner on the reverse of each photograph (not on the caption slip, in case it is removed). Self-adhesive labels are ideal. They can be obtained with your details printed in black on a white or gold background.

Safeguards for Pictures in the Post

With captions and labels in place, put your prints into a clear plastic pocket – the anti-static polypropylene kind are preferable. The benefit is twofold: in addition to giving your work a professional appearance, the pocket will provide extra protection in the post.

Illustrations in the form of 35 mm transparencies should never be submitted in a film processor's box, but in a manner that will enhance the images. The special pages which are manufactured for filing mounted transparencies are ideal. Each page comprises twenty pockets of a size to accommodate one mounted transparency. The mounts should be either card or plastic.

In no circumstances submit glass-mounted transparencies. If the glass is broken or splintered in transit, it becomes dangerous to the person who opens the package and there is also the possibility of damaging the transparency. And before buying transparency file pages, check that the materials are acid-free and are suitable for archivally safe storage. As with prints, a self-adhesive label bearing your name, address, and a copyright symbol, should be affixed on the side of the mount from which the transparency will be viewed. Some photographers who use card mounts prefer to use a rubber stamp instead of an adhesive label. With this method it is best to buy a stamp pad with quick-drying permanent ink.

Each mount should be numbered to correspond to a list of numbered captions for all the transparencies submitted. The number can be written on a self-adhesive solid circle label which should also be affixed to the mount so that it is visible when the transparency is viewed. The labels can be purchased in packs containing various colours which can be useful for filing purposes.

Transparencies are best viewed in black transparency sleeves – presentation mounts. The masks are made of heavy-duty matt black card with an aperture over which the transparency is taped. The mask is then folded and inserted into an acetate sleeve which has a clear front for viewing and a diffused back sheet, and is sealed on three sides for maximum protection. Whether viewed on a light box or hand held, the black surround isolates the image from any competing interest.

Black masks are also available in an overall size of A4 in which six 6 cm × 6 cm transparencies (very impressive owing to their size) or twenty-four 35 mm transparencies can be displayed. These are easy to view when a large number of pictures are required for a book project. They are also useful when it is important to keep transparencies in separate categories. Masks for other sizes of transparencies are also available.

When an article is accompanied by illustrations it is vital that the prints or transparencies arrive on the editor's desk in immaculate condition. After spending time and money on your manuscript and pictures, do not attempt to skimp on packaging. Always use good-quality envelopes, with your work sandwiched between rigid cardboard stiffeners.

If you use card-backed envelopes, ensure that they are of good quality and that the card is adequate for the task. If what you are mailing is especially vulnerable, it is advisable to slip in a sheet of card on the front side of a card-backed envelope for added protection.

If you need to reinforce the gummed flap of an envelope with adhesive tape, do restrict the sealing to a single strip. A package which has been over-taped can be extremely difficult to open and this increases the possibility of damaging the photographs when they are extracted. It will also distract attention from the sparkle of your presentation.

As a further safeguard, use a printed label or write the words 'photographs – please do not bend' on the outgoing and return envelopes. Remember to affix the correct postage on the self-addressed return envelope. For additional peace of mind when you mail your photographs you can choose recorded delivery or registered post.

After taking care to protect your work, ensure that it arrives in good time. From comments I have received, it is obvious that editors appreciate people who meet deadlines promptly. So if you want to establish yourself as a reliable contributor, make it a priority to despatch your words and pictures well before a magazine's deadline.

Handling Rejection

There may be occasions when despite an editor's initial positive response to your proposal, the illustrated article you had so carefully prepared and presented will be turned down. Do not take this as a personal slight. Rejection does not necessarily mean your writing and photography are not up to standard. It could be that the editor had a different approach in mind or that another article with a similar subject to yours covered the same ground. A standard rejection slip does not give you much explanation but sometimes an editor will write a few words of encouragement and explain why your work was not suitable at that particular time.

One way of responding to a rejection slip is to try contacting other publications with a similar style and content as your first target. If you receive further rejections try to put your feelings of disappointment to one side and analyse your work. Evaluate the theme and slant of the article and ascertain if the photographs enhanced the package to the degree you had originally thought. Question whether your market research had let you down. Were the pictures appropriate for the magazines you targeted?

In the early stages an editor might publish the article but not all your photographs, replacing some of your shots with other pictures. If this happens take heart; it is likely your work initially attracted the editor's attention because your submission included pictures as well as words.

If you have been unable to have an illustrated article published, do ensure that you file the photographs for possible future use. It is worth remembering, too, that one of the best ways of overcoming rejection is to be able to look forward to the acceptance of other work which you have already submitted to magazines for consideration.

6

Filing Photographs and Keeping Records

Quick-access System

From the day you start taking pictures to accompany your writing you will begin to accumulate a stock of negatives, prints and transparencies. Although it may seem convenient at the time, do not fall into the trap of leaving them in processors' wallets and boxes tucked away in a drawer until you have time to sort them out. The larger your collection becomes, the more difficult it will be to locate a particular negative or transparency. No matter how efficient your memory is, searching through an assortment of envelopes and boxes is both irksome and time-consuming. It also puts negatives and transparencies at risk from dust and finger marks.

Set up a filing system which offers quick access and adequate protection for every item. What determines how good or poor your files are, is whether you can easily retrieve any negative or transparency without ploughing through most of your collection. Just as important is to adopt a procedure that is appropriate to your requirements. So plan a system that meets your needs and can be extended to absorb subsequent growth.

Prints also require care, but if they are spoiled they can be reprinted, whereas a badly damaged negative or transparency means the loss of a precious asset. Other enemies of photographic materials are heat and damp, so keep them in cool, dry conditions. Remember, too, that the image of colour film is made of dye, so it is important to keep negatives away from the light. It is advisable when purchasing storage products to choose files of archival quality.

Whether your stock of negatives, prints or transparencies is large or small, consider it as a personal photo library and seek to extend it. Never disregard an opportunity for taking photographs for possible future use. Provided you keep your filing up to date, you should be able to locate any item of your collection without delay whenever it is required.

Protecting Your Negatives

Negatives – both black and white and colour – need to be protected from unnecessary handling, and also from abrasions caused by film surfaces rubbing together. A practical system which provides excellent long-term protection is to use loose-leaf pages with pockets to accommodate the negatives. The pages are pre-punched to fit ring-binders. It offers a choice of the number of pockets per page: 35 mm negatives which are processed by high street laboratories are usually cut into strips of four frames, and pages are available with pockets to accommodate strips of four negatives; pages to store a 36-exposure roll of 35 mm negatives are supplied with seven pockets, each of a size to accept a strip of six frames. The additional pocket can be useful if you have managed to obtain an extra shot or two out of the film.

Most writers who supply their own illustrations will probably submit photographs taken on a 35 mm camera. Whether 36- or 24-exposure films are used, the benefit of keeping negatives together and storing them as one complete film per page is that it simplifies both filing and retrieval.

If you use 120 film size the same method of page filing and storage is available for 6 cm × 6 cm negatives. A twelve-exposure roll of negatives can be filed in four strips of three frames. There are also filing pages manufactured which accommodate these larger sized negatives in three strips of four frames.

Apart from archival plastic material, storage pages are also available in transparent acetate and glassine which are acid free and suitable for long-term negative storage. Glassine is a translucent paper and therefore not clear enough to examine negatives filed in the pockets. This need not be a disadvantage provided you can refer to a contact sheet for any assessment.

If you have an APS camera ensure that each cartridge in which the negatives are returned is always given the same reference number as the accompanying photo index print. This is necessary for filing and storage purposes.

Contact Prints

A 36-exposure film cut into strips of six frames is just right for producing a 10 in × 8 in contact print. When you take a black and white film for processing, include a written order with the film requesting a contact print and for your negatives to be cut into strips of six frames. This will give you thirty-six

The Dome of the Rock with columns in the foreground that partially frame the colourful tiles and grained marble. The golden dome completes the picture. A human figure in the lower third of the photograph establishes scale but is in a position which does not intrude or detract from the colour and detail

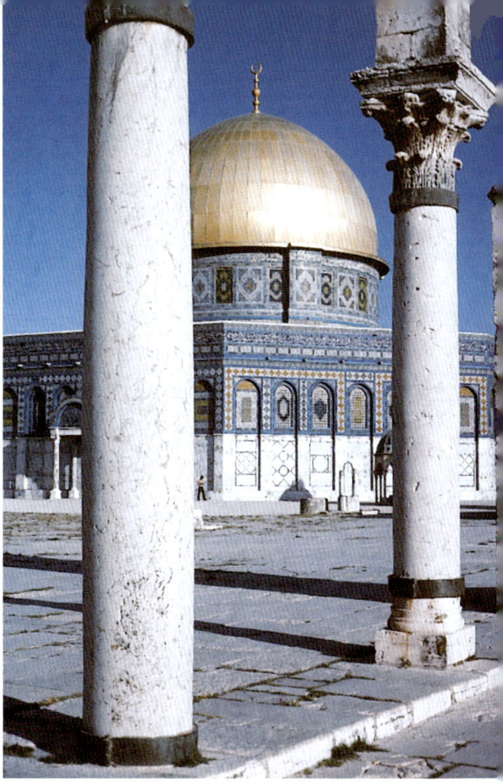

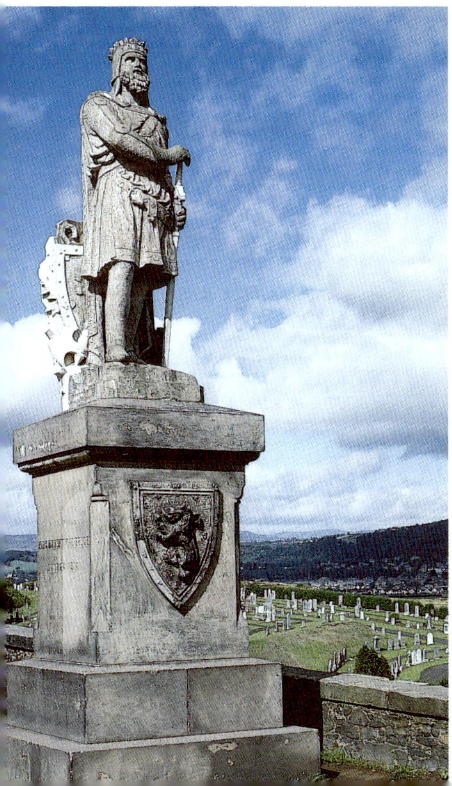

If you include a statue of someone relevant to the period when illustrating an historical article, it can complement the factual details. The memorial to Robert Bruce stands at Stirling Castle and benefits from being photographed against a bright sky and by not having to compete with a background of buildings

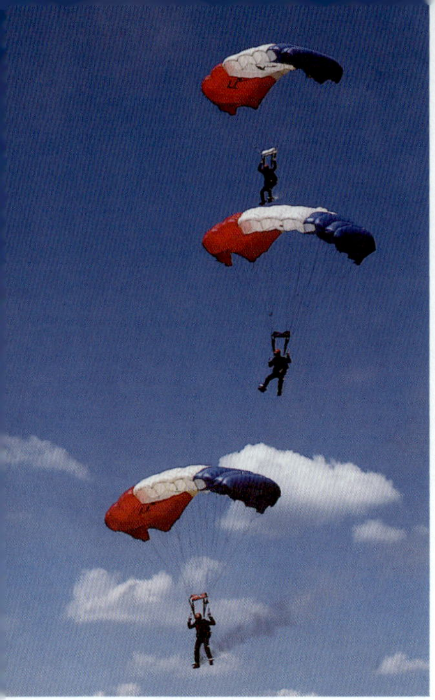

When following action through your viewfinder make every effort to keep the camera steady. Ensure that you do not jerk the shutter release. If you are photographing a subject such as a free-fall parachute display team, focus on two or three parachutists and take several pictures as they glide to the ground

Mock battles take place regularly up and down the country. Enthusiasts dressed in authentic costumes re-enact events of the Civil War. With conflicts going on all over the battlefield, photograph as many as possible, but concentrate your lens on one group at a time. I was able to frame the pikemen tightly in a skirmish with the aid of a 35 mm SLR and a 75–150 zoom lens

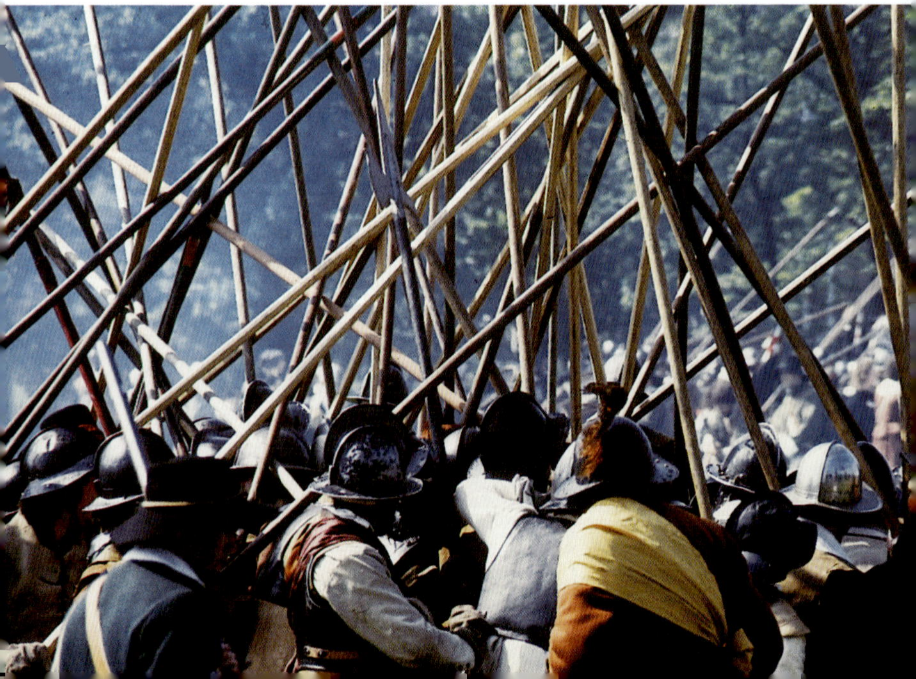

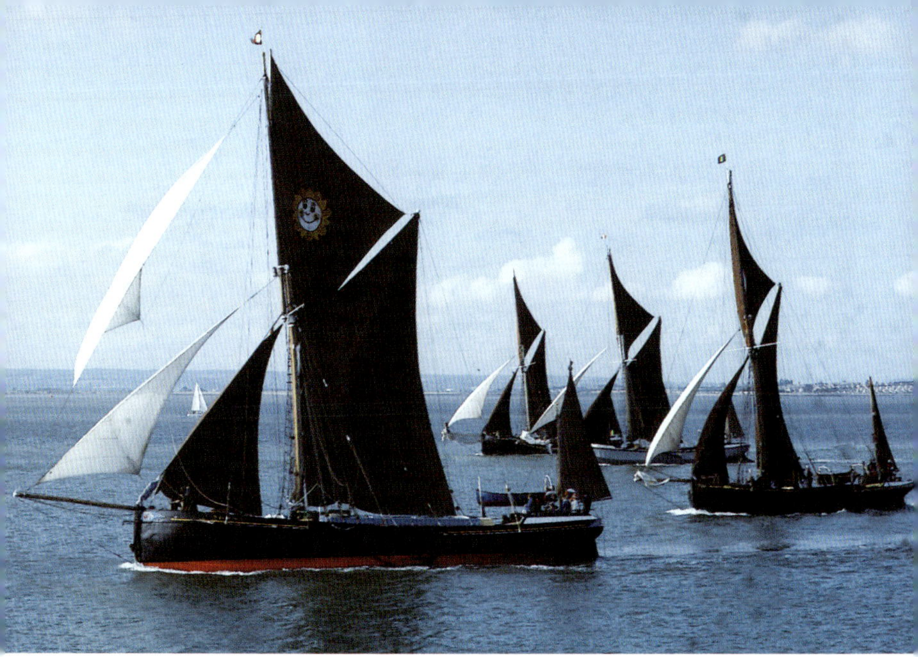

These majestic sailing barges were competing in an annual race on the River Thames. To get a picture of several craft together you need to be present at the start of a race because such a formation does not last for long. A zoom lens enabled me to fill the frame

This picture requires no second glance to confirm its autumnal theme. To emphasize the subject it was necessary to move in close to eliminate competing interest. This is the type of subject that you should try to make time for, even if you are seeking pictures for a different theme

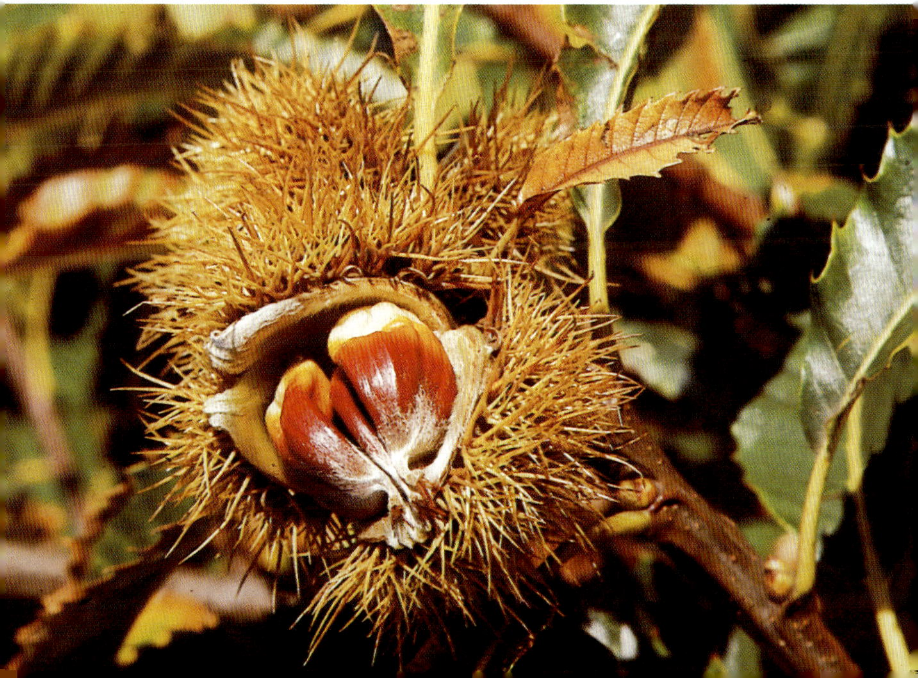

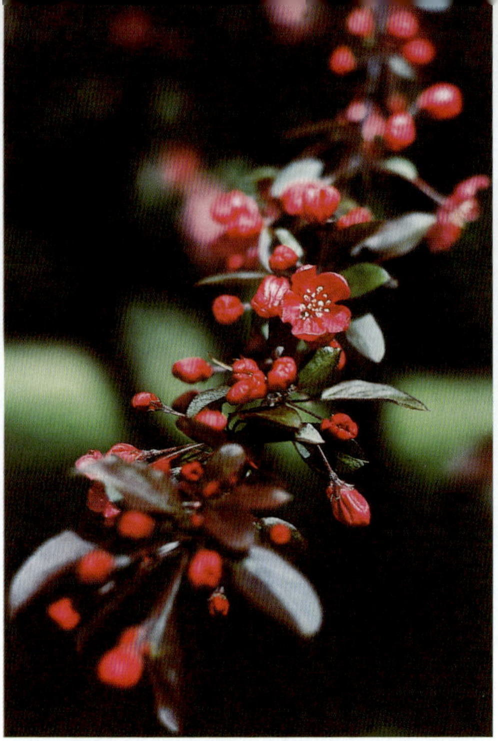

For this shot the lens was focused on the only open bloom. It is a good example of how much shallower the depth of field is at a close focusing distance. One method of increasing the depth of field would have been to use a smaller aperture, which would have required a slower shutter speed to maintain correct exposure

The interior of the church was decorated for harvest festival and a hay cart was prominently displayed in the church grounds. Situated in Constable country it was a reminder of the famous artist's work, 'The Haywain'. For this shot the hay cart became the major subject matter, with the church serving as a backdrop

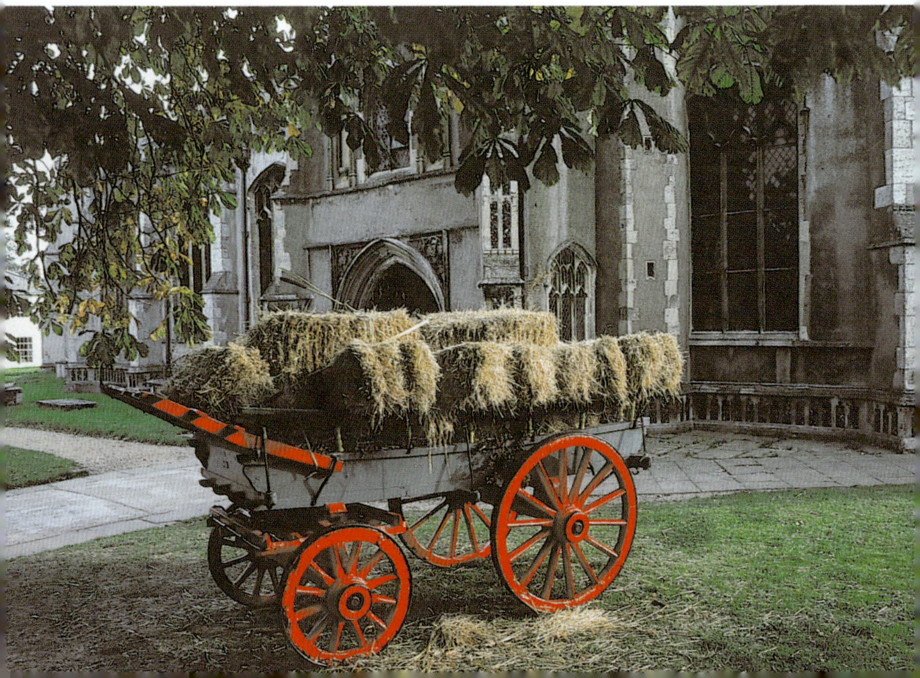

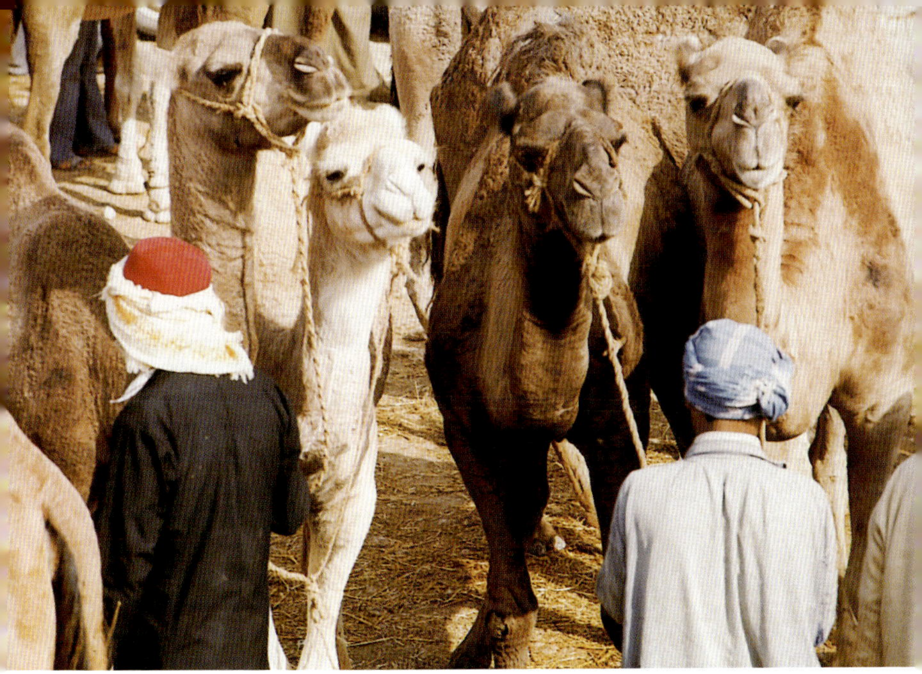

When visiting a Tunisian camel market I quickly discovered people and camels, but not much space. Finding a vantage point allowed me to photograph an overview of the market but the excitement and activity seem too far removed. It was only when I moved among the crowd and the animals that I was able to capture pictures which represented the market atmosphere

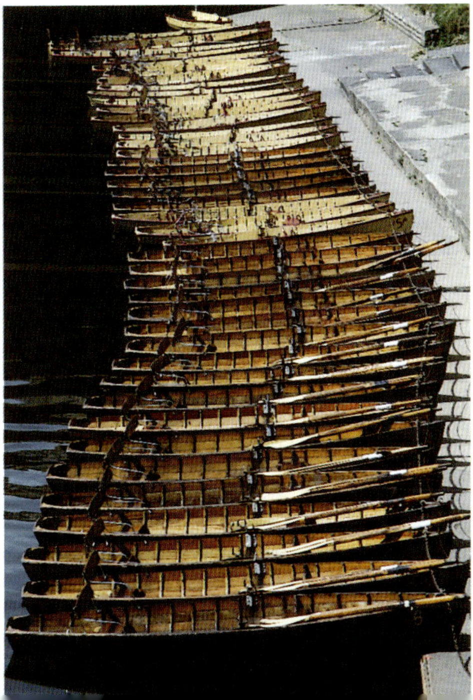

The striking repetition of shapes formed by a row of pleasure boats was photographed early morning before visitors arrived. This type of picture is always worth taking to place in your file for possible future use – perhaps as an illustration for a leisure or river feature

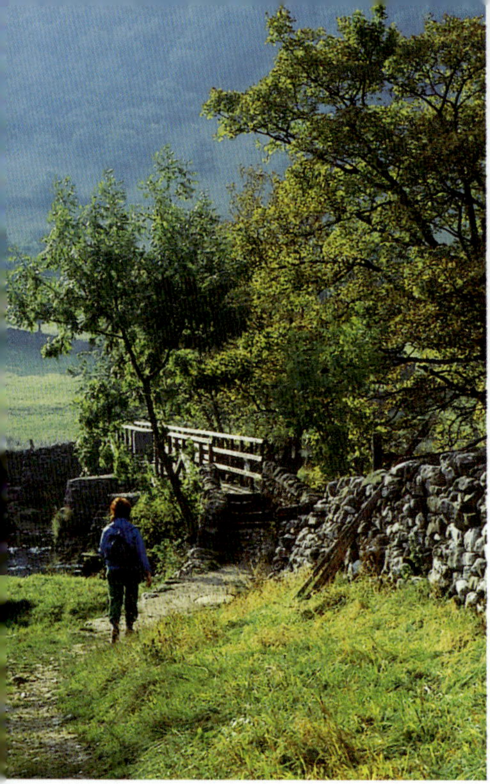

Illustrated articles for magazines featuring an outdoor pursuit such as walking are enhanced by pictures of the landscape. However, it is important that a good proportion of the photographs include human interest. Although the lone hiker does not occupy a large part of the composition in this shot, if you cover the area the picture loses the significance human interest provides

Whether you are taking pictures of farming implements from previous centuries or other relics from the past, do not lose sight of the need for good picture arrangement. If your photographs are mainly of individual items endeavour to vary the selection and include pictures with more than one piece of equipment. When visiting castles or landscaped gardens keep a look out for subjects that will give variety to your range of pictures

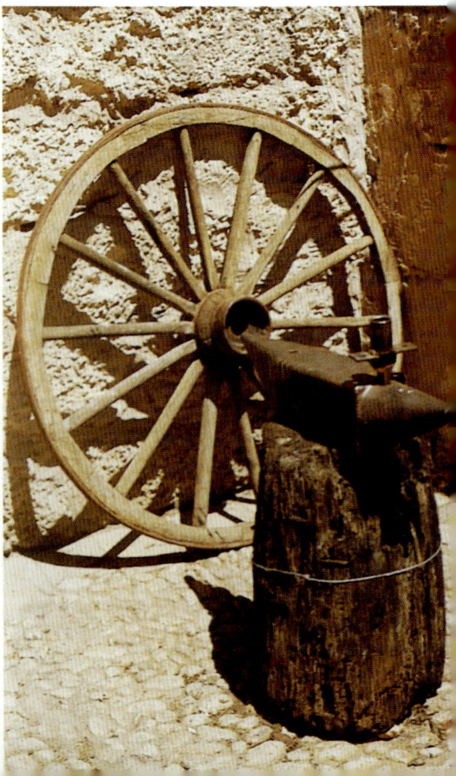

The two towers in the photo were retained as possible mausoleums when the remainder of the church was demolished. However, they stand as a memorial to an idea unfulfilled. It is the sort of subject that might form an illustrated article for a county magazine. Rather than being satisfied with a straight-on shot, take time and try alternative viewpoints that will suggest the character and history of a building

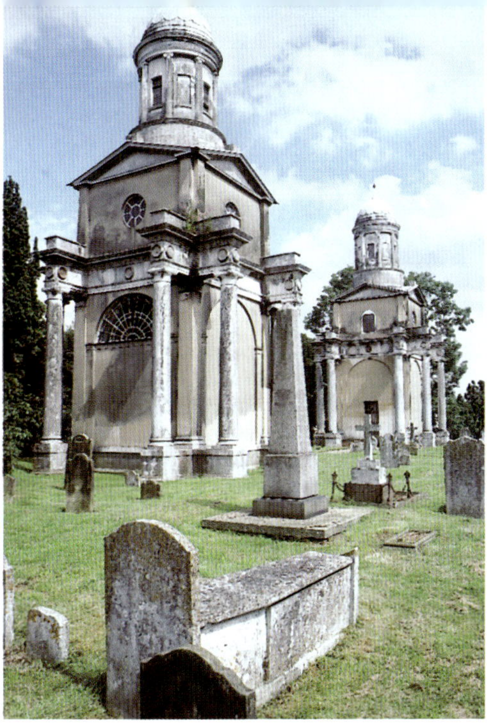

Photographed at Studley Royal, Yorkshire, in evening light, this is an example of the value of foreground interest balancing the overall scene. The ripples in the water break up the reflection of the Temple of Piety and on this occasion spoil any chance of a mirror-like image but the scene is improved by the inclusion of the ornamental feature on the right-hand side of the picture

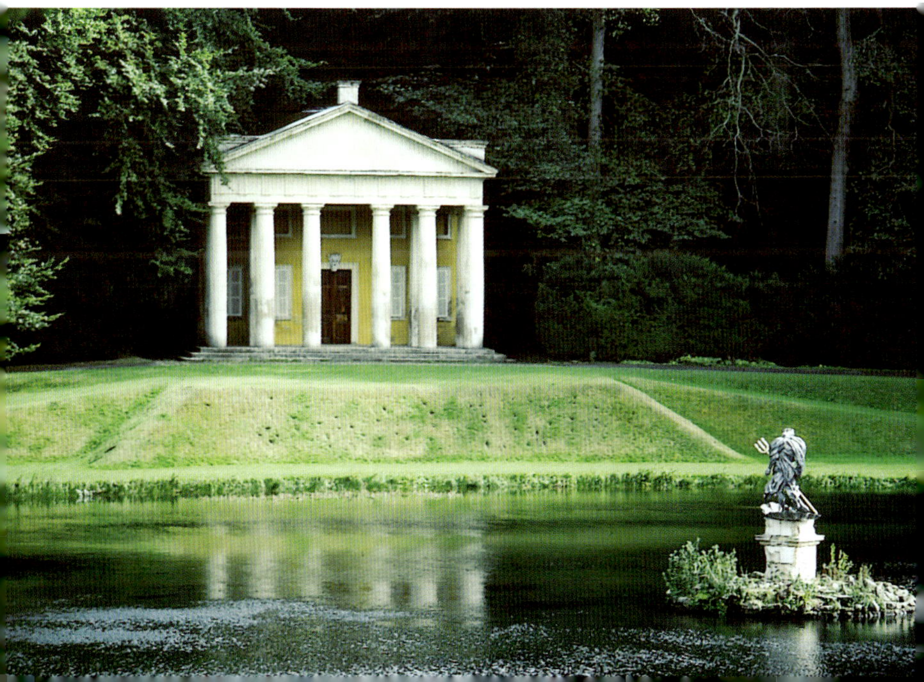

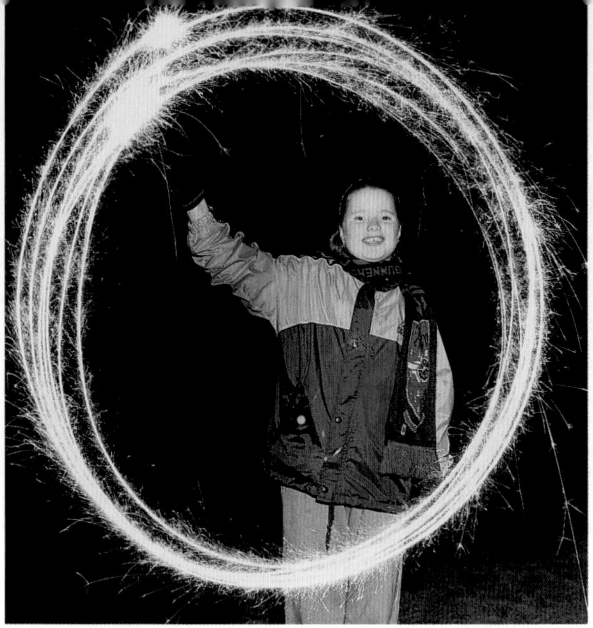

The idea is not original but it is a striking alternative to fireworks shooting skyward and could easily take its place among shots for a bonfire night article. A 10-second exposure was given to capture the sparkler's movement. A flashgun was fired to illuminate the girl prior to the shutter being closed. Film speed: ISO 100

This photograph was taken to accompany a festive article and was shot on a manual 35 mm SLR with the flashgun set on auto. The flash was bounced from the ceiling. Although I took pictures from different flash-to-subject distances the flashgun's sensor produced the correct illumination. Relying on auto-flash enabled me to concentrate on focusing and on the youngsters' expressions

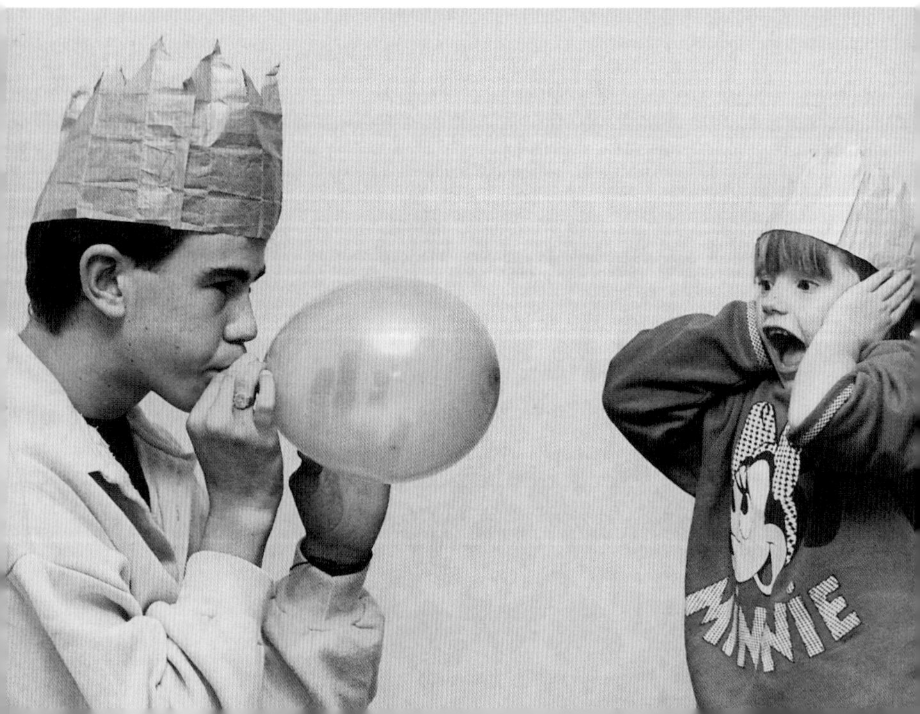

pictures, the same size as the negatives, reproduced in six rows on one sheet of photographic paper, which you can examine before selecting shots for enlargement. The contact print can be filed as a valuable reference in your filing system.

An additional service provided by colour processing laboratories is a photo index print of a processed 35 mm film. This displays every image and the negative number for reference purposes. It is similar to the photo index prints supplied with processed APS films. Although the pictures are smaller than the same sized images of a 35 mm black and white contact print, for a small charge you can have a complete record for your files.

Individual Reference Numbers

Storing contact and photo index prints in separate files from negatives avoids pages of negatives being handled unnecessarily when you are looking for a particular image. It is imperative that both the contact or photo index print and its negative page are numbered identically and that the negative pages are filed in numerical order. For retrieval purposes each negative should be known by its frame number, which is located on the edge of the film and which will be reproduced on the contact or photo index print. So, for example, if we refer to the first roll of thirty-six negatives as 'film 1' and an enlargement is required of the eighth negative on the roll, then the negative reference number would be 1/8. Reference 18/32 would refer to negative 32 of film 18, and so on.

Keep the system simple by marking film reference numbers clearly on all contact prints and negative pages in the following style: 18/1–36 or 18/1–24, indicating the number of the film and its number of frames. The letter 'C' can be added to denote colour film and 'B' for black and white.

The reference numbers can be written with an all-surface pen which is suitable for writing on plastic surfaces and resin-coated photographic paper. This type of pen is especially useful for recording information on the reverse side of a contact or index print. The details should include the date when the pictures were taken, a record of pictures submitted and published, suggestions for captions, and other facts of possible value for future occasions.

This procedure should be quite adequate for those whose photography is secondary to writing. Obviously for someone with an output involving a very large number of negatives covering a wide range of subjects, a more extensive classification would be needed.

As your stock of negatives increases, contact sheets can be filed in separate ring-binders in chronological order or divided into subject categories such as animals, landscapes, people, etc., but this will depend on the variety and kind of subjects in your collection.

A Card Index or Computer Database

It is helpful to add a card index or computer database (one is included in Microsoft Works, for instance) to your system if sets of negatives include more than one subject category. The index or database then becomes a central point for details of all your files, and the information enables you to locate any negative or transparency quickly. With each frame individually numbered, any image can be retrieved by referring to the subject on the index or database. The sections in the system can be determined by the subjects which comprise the bulk of your photography. Categories could be based on the following, with the first letter of the section's name serving as a prefix to the negative number for record purposes:

A – animals
B – buildings
L – landscape
M – miscellaneous
P – people
S – sport

If you specialize in a category, such as buildings for example, the section could be subdivided as follows:

B1 – castles
B2 – churches
B3 – houses
B4 – inns

This also shows how the system can be expanded when a section becomes too full; it can be rearranged without any disruption to the negative files. There is no universal system which will suit everyone but this can be adapted to your needs. Card indexing or a computer database are particularly useful for cross-referencing when, for instance, a picture which includes a vehicle and a building needs to be listed under more than one category.

The overriding consideration is to maintain a filing system which can function without the need to reorganize your entire collection of negatives whenever it becomes necessary to subdivide certain subjects.

Protecting Your Transparencies

Transparencies can be filed in a similar way except that the pages will comprise rows of separate pockets which will each accommodate a mounted 35 mm transparency. These pages are also pre-punched to fit ring-binders. The transparencies can be grouped according to subject, which makes viewing easier when comparing pictures. Each mount should be numbered and a card index or a database used for recording dates and picture details.

Filing transparencies in pages is preferable to storing them in boxes, as the pages allow a quick review of the subject matter. This eliminates the chore of having to remove them individually from the boxes.

If possible store ring-binders upright or with the spine uppermost, in order to prevent undue pressure on negatives and transparencies. Wherever you keep your files it is worthwhile placing a few sachets of silica gel nearby to absorb any moisture.

Having gone to the trouble of diligently filing and indexing, it is imperative that you keep a record of any item removed from the files. It is also essential that all negatives and transparencies are returned to the correct file after use.

A Light Box

If you are handling transparencies on a regular basis, using a light box is the best way to assess the images and to sort them for filing. It will also make life easier when you are examining negatives. A range of light boxes is available including 'daylight' versions, which are illuminated by colour corrected fluorescent tubes which give a reliable representation of colour. For viewing fine detail you will also need a loupe or a good-quality magnifying glass.

Storing Prints

Prints do not require such detailed classification but should be filed in subject categories. If you can obtain some photographic printing paper boxes they are excellent for storing prints, but document wallets are a good substitute. Try to get used to writing the negative number on the reverse of all photographs you send out with a manuscript. The reference should also be recorded with the details of the article which the prints accompany.

Digital Files and Photo CDs

Digital camera owners also need the assurance of a safe storage system for their pictures. A Photo CD is not only good for storage, but it will also free up valuable space on a computer's hard drive, and avoid the possibility of losing images if you suffer a hard drive breakdown.

A CD-writer enables you to store your digital images. Writable CDs can file a hundred or more high-resolution pictures. If you wish, you can make an additional copy of each disc as a safeguard in the event of a CD being accidentally damaged. Ensure that all Photo CDs are numbered and descriptions of the pictures are filed.

As we saw in chapter 5, computer users can also order a Photo CD with their negative processing and colour prints, giving a viewable digital record of their shots as well as a set of thumbnail images on a print. In addition, digital enlargements can be made when required via an inkjet printer.

Copyright

You should be aware of copyright protection. Over the years a number of amendments have been made to the British copyright law. Unless you have assigned the copyright of a literary work to a publisher, the copyright belongs to you as the author of a manuscript. Similarly, as the photographer, you own the copyright to your pictures. There are exceptions to this rule: for example, if the pictures were taken by you as an employee in the course of your employment. There are also complications if the film was purchased by a person other than the photographer.

When you submit any picture for possible publication, ensure that the copyright symbol (©) appears on the reverse side of all prints and on every transparency mount. The symbol should be connected clearly with the name of the author. For example: 'Copyright © 2002 Jim Jones', or 'Photo © Jim Jones 2002'. The symbol can be conveniently included on your name and address label and serve as a permanent reminder to whoever is reproducing your photograph that you are the owner of the copyright.

Generally, when a previously unpublished manuscript is submitted to a magazine, the author offers what are called first British serial rights. The rights offered when photographs are submitted – whether accompanying an article or not – are single reproduction rights. It is not necessary to stipulate this, as it is accepted practice. It allows the magazine to use each picture once only.

Following publication, you are free to submit the photographs elsewhere. Obviously you should allow some time to elapse before doing so, and it would be sensible not to send identical images to the editor of a competing publication; this would be one way to get yourself remembered rather too well! Keeping details of every photograph that is submitted for publication will help to avoid that kind of error.

Some photographs can continue to earn reproduction fees for a number of years, sometimes from the same magazine. Pictures of mine have been retained following the initial publication and republished over several years. So be wary of any request for you to sign away the full copyright of a picture. If you are tempted, you should only agree provided a substantial fee is offered or you have other negatives of the subject on file.

Model Release Forms

A model release form is primarily a contract between a photographer and a model. The form is signed by the model who consents to be photographed, and depending on the wording of the form, agrees to the pictures being used in a particular way. Therefore, if a photographer hires a person to ride a certain make of bicycle for a series of pictures, for example, the cyclist's fee is basically a wage for his or her time. A signed release means the photographs can be used for the specified purpose without further permission, provided they do not bring the person into disrepute and the result is not offensive. If the photographs are used for a purpose not indicated on the model release form the person can sue the photographer or at least claim a further fee.

Putting your family or friends in your pictures when human interest is required is an alternative to hiring models, and in most cases people will agree to be photographed provided the pictures will not be used in a discreditable way.

Although there should be no problem in taking photographs in public generally, if someone is easily identifiable and particularly prominent in a picture, a signed release form would probably be required if the photograph was eventually placed with a picture library or agency. Before you hand over a signed model release form to a picture library or agency, or to anyone else, obtain a photocopy for your records.

A helpful book which addresses copyright and other legal matters concerning photography is *The Photographer & the Law* (BFP Books).

Systematic Records

A record book should include the name of the magazine receiving your work, the negative/transparency number, the date when the picture was submitted, the dates when accepted, rejected, published or returned, the title of the manuscript it illustrated, and the payment received.

The Inland Revenue may be interested in your extra income, so accurate records are essential. These details could just as easily be kept on your computer, on index cards or on a combined manuscript/picture record. But whichever method you use, the important thing is to keep the system up to date. Provided entries are made on a regular basis, you will always know exactly the whereabouts of any negative, print or transparency.

Other Outlets for Your Pictures

As your picture file expands, certain photographs which are surplus to current projects will stand out because of their impact. This can prompt the question whether they could be profitably used elsewhere. If you find yourself in that situation the following outlets are worth considering, provided the specific requirements can be met.

Postcards

The picture postcard trade has grown immensely over the last few years. In addition to traditional holiday view cards, a variety of images in colour, and also black and white, are extremely popular. Some of the pictures are also reproduced as posters.

The secret of getting photographs accepted is to know exactly what publishers are seeking. Look in galleries and shops to find out what is currently popular. Publishers differ in both style and choice of subjects, and competition is fierce. If your pictures are to be considered they should be appropriate to the latest designs being produced.

Much depends on the kind of photographs you take. If, for example, you have a number of vintage car pictures on file which are carefully composed, pin sharp and well printed on glossy paper, then obviously you would need to find a publisher whose series of postcards included cars.

The range of subjects published is usually evocative, moody or cute. Humour also has its place. Try to send a number of photographs for consideration rather than a single example. It is also an advantage to use your writing skills to provide informative or witty captions which are relevant to the pictures.

The usual reasons for rejection by postcard publishers are that the pictures are not in keeping with the style of image required and that the contributor has not taken note of the existing range of postcards.

Greetings Cards

The requirements of publishers of greetings cards are entirely different from the postcard market. First, transparencies are preferred. Some publishers specify sizes of 6 cm × 6 cm or larger, but many will consider 35 mm provided they are of the highest quality. You must know exactly the type of subjects the publisher seeks.

Greetings card publishers normally use more artwork images than photographs and many also carry illustrations reproduced from paintings, but there are openings for good colour shots. A review of those on sale will reveal the usual visual clichés, but there is obviously a demand for these. Designs are available for every occasion, ranging from anniversary to get well and thank you cards. Animals, colourful gardens, flowers and thatched cottages are still bestsellers.

Any pictures you submit should be something more than a straightforward shot. Special lighting effects, a striking arrangement and an unusual angle will lift a subject out of the conventional mode.

Publishers of postcards and greetings cards usually buy the rights for exclusive use of a picture for an agreed period. The photographer retains the copyright and is free to offer the image to a non-competitive market later.

Calendars

Looking around book shops and stationers, you can compare the calendars on offer. Make a note of the publishers' names and the kind of pictures they use. There is always a variety of formats on display, with animals, landscapes and famous landmarks among the popular subjects, but it is not easy to break into the market.

Almost all calendar pictures are reproduced from transparencies. Until a few years ago nothing smaller than a 5 in × 4 in transparency was considered by many publishers. Although some still stipulate that size as a minimum, the majority will accept 6 cm × 6 cm and some companies will consider 35 mm transparencies provided they are of a very high standard.

To be in with a chance of getting your work accepted, transparencies must be blemish free and display good colour saturation. The image should be sharply focused and correctly exposed. Apart from technical qualities the pictures must be eye-catching. If you consider you have pictures which compare favourably with published examples, then write a letter of enquiry to the calendar company to whom your work seems appropriate.

Photographic Competitions

A frequently overlooked outlet for pictures is the photo competition. Approaching this opportunity thoughtfully and seeing it as a challenge raises your standard of work and increases your chances of gaining a prize. Prizes are offered in the form of cash and equipment in numerous competitions which are announced throughout the year. Photography magazines are an obvious place to find them; they not only announce their own contests but sometimes inform their readers of competitions sponsored by other organizations.

Of course there are many other places to look.

Manufacturers, travel companies and the media are frequently involved in the sponsorship of photographic competitions. Details may be found in display advertisements, obscure paragraphs and editorial columns in newspapers and magazines. Another source is the local supermarket. Food cartons and confectionery packets are all possible carriers of competition details.

When a contest is announced read the rules very carefully and ensure that you abide by them. Many pictures fail because the entrants did not follow the rules. Note the maximum and minimum sizes of prints and transparencies permitted, and give yourself a better chance by submitting the largest size the rules allow. Also observe the final day for receiving entries and post your picture well in advance of the closing date.

Most competitions are run fairly and are beyond reproach. However, any contest with rules stating that non-winning entries may be retained for possible use by the sponsors without payment should be avoided.

When you plan to take pictures for a competition, make a list of your ideas before you start. Usually the first few suggestions that come to mind can be disregarded, as most other entrants are also likely to have thought of them. Do comply with the theme of the competition. No matter how excellent a photograph may be, if it does not conform to the title of the contest, it is a waste of everyone's time and money.

One way of pleasing the judges and tipping the balance in your favour is to present the subject matter in an interesting and creative manner. If the rules do not state that your entry has to be taken during the period of the competition, you can look through your existing prints and negatives for a likely picture.

If your picture has the impact the sponsors seek and it

reaches the final selection, make sure you do not lose out through poor presentation. When the winners are being chosen the surviving pictures will be closely scrutinized; damaged corners will be even more apparent and detract from the picture's appeal. Sometimes winning pictures are displayed or reproduced in the press, so it is unlikely that a badly creased print would stand much chance. As always, present your pictures in the best possible way and ensure that they are adequately protected.

Picture Libraries and Agencies

The majority of picture libraries and agencies that provide a service for the publishing industry deal exclusively in colour transparencies, although some also handle black and white prints. Although colour prints are now being considered for publication more than they were, not many agents are prepared to accept them.

If you want to try to place your work with a picture library or agency you must first find a company which handles your type of pictures. Some specialize in one or two categories, whereas others cover a wide range of subjects. The first step is to contact an agency and request information about their working procedure. Requirements vary, but an agency is likely to ask for an initial submission of somewhere between 50 and 300 pictures. If your work is acceptable they will probably expect a supply of a hundred or more pictures on a regular basis.

Your pictures are likely to be retained for a minimum period of three to five years in order to give your material maximum market exposure. Do not expect much return in the first year or so, but consider the arrangement as an ongoing investment.

Picture libraries and agencies work on a commission of around 50 per cent, which may sound high. However, when you consider their overheads, their knowledge of the market and the costs, filing, cataloguing and making your pictures available for distribution, the figure begins to look more reasonable.

Unless you can supply a large number of pictures frequently, this outlet is not for you. For an agency to handle twenty of your best shots would not justify the expense involved. Nevertheless, if you specialize in a subject and have a substantial selection of transparencies, then you may be able to interest an agency in your material. But before making contact you should ensure that your pictures are of a high quality and that you have accurate details of the places and subjects of each image.

Details of card and calendar publishers, and of picture libraries and agencies, can be found in the *Writers' & Artists' Yearbook* (A. & C. Black) and in *The Freelance Photographer's Market Handbook* (BFP Books). Picture libraries are also featured in *The Writer's Handbook* (Macmillan). These publications are available in bookshops and public libraries.

7
Home Processing

There are bound to be times when you will collect a set of prints from the processing laboratory only to discover that not all the pictures are as you visualized them. With the wide availability of colour processing, it is possible that some causes of disappointment can be rectified by a reprint. However, when the photographs are black and white and prints are required quickly, a speedy turn-round is unlikely to be possible.

If you had a scanner and an inkjet printer with your computer, you could digitize the pictures that required improving (as explained in chapter 5), make the necessary changes and produce the reprints on high gloss photo quality paper. But if the necessary digital equipment is not for you at present but your output of black and white photographs is reasonably high, you might want a darkroom. This would enable you to also make certain improvements, perhaps by giving the main interest more impact by extra enlargement, or by directing attention to the subject by excluding distracting detail from the edges of the frame.

Whether you decide to carry out your own developing and printing will depend on the kind of photographs you take, whether you are concerned about taking up time which could be used for writing and how much money you wish to spend on equipment. Another consideration is the amount of vacant space in your home which could be used for darkroom work.

As I have said, some of the illustrations required for general articles are likely to be black and white, so working in this medium is a good place to start. The following advice therefore applies mainly to black and white processing. And if you do not want to get involved with developing prints, but would simply like the option of processing a film urgently when the need arises, a darkroom is not a requirement.

Film Processing in Daylight

If you do not have a darkroom and do not want to have to black out a room whenever you load a film into a developing tank, you can use a changing bag which is made of a light-proof material and is double-zipped. Sleeves with elastic cuffs allow you to load an exposed film on to the tank's spiral – a reel with grooves to retain the film – without any danger of stray light fogging the film.

Once the loading is complete the tank can be removed from the changing bag and the film processing can be done in ordinary room lighting. Daylight developing tanks for films are made of plastic or stainless steel. A light-trapped opening in the lid permits the chemicals to be poured in and out.

In addition to a changing bag and developing tank, you will need chemicals, plastic graduates for preparing and accurately measuring the processing solutions, a large jug, a funnel, a timer, thermometer, film clips and perhaps a washing hose.

Producing Contact Prints

If you want to go a stage further and make a contact print from the developed film, this process has to be carried out in a room illuminated only by a safelight. The strips of negatives to be exposed on to a sheet of photographic paper are inserted into a contact printing frame, or alternatively are held in contact with the photographic paper with a sheet of clear glass.

Exposure can be provided by momentarily switching on the room light. The exposed paper is then processed in special dishes successively – developer, stop bath and fixer – and the print is then washed in running water before hanging it up to dry. See the section on essential accessories later in this chapter for dish sizes and print tongs.

A Temporary Darkroom

When enlargements are to be produced, darkroom facilities are needed. Although an ideal solution would be to convert an unused room into a darkroom, complete with a sink and running water, it is not a prerequisite. You can, with care, arrange a temporary darkroom in a bathroom or kitchen. The more space you have to work in the easier it will be to set up, but it is surprising what can be done in a confined area.

A bathroom is convenient, as you will have water on hand. A large board placed over the bath will provide an ample work surface for processing dishes, and a small cupboard or table would support an enlarger. For safety reasons, power for the enlarger should come from a point outside the bathroom. Use a waterproof covering to protect surfaces and the floor from chemical splashes.

Depending on the type of house, a little-used loft conversion could provide a more permanently equipped place, although it might be too hot in the summer or too cold in the winter.

One photographer improvised a darkroom in a corner of a large room. It occupied an area roughly 6 ft square. The walls comprised a timber framework covered on both sides with hardboard. The outer surface was decorated to match the room. A well-planned layout ensured that no space was wasted, but the area was not uncomfortable to work in. Although no running water was available, processed prints were dropped into a bucket of water and taken elsewhere in the house for a final wash at the conclusion of each printing session.

If these suggestions are not appropriate to your circumstances and you have a few hundred pounds to invest, the answer might be a portable darkroom tent – a lightproof fabric cubicle supported on a metal frame which can be assembled in minutes.

Blackout Material

Whether a darkroom is temporary or permanent, a basic requirement is the ability to exclude all stray light from the room. Large windows can be blacked out by assembling a softwood frame fitted with a sheet of hardboard that is cut to a size to fit within the window recess. The edges of the frame should be covered with thick fabric to serve as a light-trap.

For permanent darkroom light-proofing, blinds and fittings can be obtained from photographic suppliers, made to your individual specifications. For temporary window blackout a black vinyl material is available which will adhere to a glass surface by static electricity. No adhesive is involved, it is easily attached to the window by using a squeegee or your hands, and it can be used repeatedly without any loss in its effectiveness.

To test how light-proof any blackout material is, turn off the light and sit in the room for about ten minutes to become fully accustomed to the darkness. Any light leaks will gradually become discernible. Black-out foam strips can be affixed to the door frame to prevent light coming through gaps around the door and fogging film or printing paper.

Safety in the Darkroom

It is absolutely essential that electricity and water are kept well apart. Ensure that there is a dry bench for the enlarger, negatives and printing paper, and a wet bench for chemicals and processing dishes. Apart from safety, using two benches will also prevent negatives and unused paper being affected by chemical splashes from the dishes. Clean all surfaces at the close of each working session.

If your working space does not allow you to have independent benches, separate the wet and dry areas with a sturdy partition. Check that electrical equipment is properly earthed and that there is no frayed wiring. Never touch any plugs, switches or electrical equipment with wet hands.

Provided a darkroom is effectively blacked out, it is not

necessary to paint the walls and ceiling in a dark colour. Light-coloured walls will help to reflect the illumination from the safelight around the room. The only area where dark paint would be beneficial is the section of the wall adjacent to the enlarger, where a coat of matt black will prevent stray light from the enlarger reflecting back on to the printing paper on the baseboard.

When setting up a darkroom of any size, remember that dust is a deadly enemy, so it is worthwhile having smooth surfaces for easy cleaning. Adequate ventilation is also very important, especially when chemicals are being used. Some bathrooms are fitted with an extractor fan which will provide the necessary change of air.

When a temporary set-up does not have a sink it is preferable to mix and dilute any chemicals before bringing them into the darkroom. Follow the manufacturer's instructions carefully. Be safety conscious. When mixing chemicals with water, pour the chemical into the water, rather than adding water to the chemical. Ensure that mixing is carried out in a well-ventilated area. Store all chemicals in clearly labelled bottles and place them safely out of the reach of children.

Choosing an Enlarger

The enlarger is your main piece of equipment. Making an enlargement involves placing the negative into a carrier and projecting the image on to a sensitized sheet of printing paper. The sizing of the image is done by adjusting the height of the enlarger head.

Before purchasing an enlarger think carefully about your aims. If you do not want to venture into colour at all, then you need only look at black and white models, but it is better to purchase a colour enlarger from the start if you intend either to get involved with colour printing some time in the future or to make black and white prints on 'variable contrast' black and white paper – which requires the light from the enlarger's lamp to be colour-filtered.

A number of models, especially those in the lower price range, are available with a lens. Provided it is not a budget-price lens and you do not require prints larger than 10 in × 8 in, the results from such an enlarger should be satisfactory. But remember that a lens is the most important component of an enlarger, just as it is with a camera. The sharpness of the overall image will depend on the quality of the lens. Buying a cheap enlarger lens is false economy. It will never do justice to the results of a good camera lens, so buy the very best you can afford.

An enlarger also needs to be rigid so that it remains vibration-free when in use. Controls should be easily accessible under safelight conditions. The focusing mechanism must operate smoothly and precisely, and the enlarger lamp should provide even illumination over the entire picture area. These considerations are important when you are producing pictures for publication. When buying an enlarger, request a demonstration with the lens fitted and note the height of the column, which will determine how large an image can be projected on to the baseboard.

Essential Accessories

Having considered the most expensive part of your darkroom, the remaining necessities will not be too hard on your bank balance. In addition to the items for processing I have already referred to, your shopping list should include a set of three 10 in × 8 in dishes for developer, stop bath and fixer, together with three print tongs for transferring prints from dish to dish.

To avoid the risk of cross-contamination of the chemicals, mark the dishes with a waterproof pen or buy a colour-coded set. You will also need a plastic waste bin for the discarded test strips and reject prints.

Colour prints can be developed in a dish or a print processing drum. A drum is used in a similar way to a film processing tank, with the exposed printing paper being loaded into the drum in total darkness before the development process is carried out in normal room lighting. Dish development must take place in total darkness.

Both time and temperature have to be carefully observed in most aspects of darkroom operations. A good-quality timer and thermometer are therefore essential for maintaining accuracy when films are processed or prints are developed. Exposing a picture on the enlarger baseboard also requires precise timing. Using a timer with a clear audible signal will be indispensable at the enlarging stage. Alternatively, buy an automatic timer which counts down a preset period and then turns off the enlarger lamp.

If your enlarger does not have an automatic focusing system, a focus finder – sometimes referred to as a focusing magnifier – will ensure that a negative is focused satisfactorily on the enlarger baseboard. When it is positioned on the masking frame you view a portion of the projected image through an eyepiece which enables you to focus on the tiny grain structure of the negative. The enlarger's focusing control is adjusted until the grain comes into sharp focus.

Another small but useful aid is a blower brush for removing

dust that has settled on the negative. A masking frame will also prove its worth. It can be set to accommodate whatever paper size is being used, and will keep the paper flat and in position on the enlarger baseboard. It will also ensure a clean white border on the edges of the photograph when required.

You will also need a good safelight, which can be bench- or wall-mounted, but must be of a colour to which the materials are insensitive. Paper for black and white printing can be safely handled under a safelight, but check the manufacturer's recommendations as to the minimum safelight-to-paper distance and the colour (red or orange, for instance) of the illumination. When it is necessary to change a safelight bulb, always make sure that the replacement is the correct wattage.

Make a list of the items you need and compare prices before you commit yourself to expensive purchases. Other equipment such as a dishwarmer to keep the print developing dish at a constant temperature, film and print dryers, and an auto print-washer unit can be added at a later date.

You can keep equipment clean and protected from dust when not in use with polythene bags. This also helps to reduce the need for dusting when preparing for a film processing or printing session. Use a vacuum cleaner for general cleaning. Any chemical splashes should be wiped away immediately and not left to dry out. A fan could make your darkroom cooler in hot weather, but may increase dust problems.

Starter Kits

For those who prefer to buy the equipment as a complete package, there are a number of reasonably priced darkroom starter kits available. An outfit for black and white photography, excluding enlarger and lens, contains all you need to launch into darkroom work, including chemicals, fifty sheets of 10 in × 8 in printing paper, as well as two rolls of black and white film to get you motivated. Alternatively, you can go for a basic home darkroom outfit, complete with an enlarger and lens, and all the major items you are likely to require.

An outfit to set you up for colour processing and printing, comprising an enlarger, a lens, a starter pack of chemicals and colour printing paper, is also available. Although it is promoted for colour processing, it can also be used with the appropriate materials to produce black and white work.

Purchasing any of these kits is just one way of acquiring basic equipment, but do not make the mistake of buying a complete outfit which contains items that you are unlikely to use. Any good photographic dealer will be able to advise on the choice of enlargers and darkroom accessories which are the most appropriate for your requirements.

Producing Black and White Prints

A darkroom of your own gives you the advantage of processing a film or developing a print at short notice. You can also size and improve the appearance of a picture. An over- or underdeveloped black and white negative can often be rectified by careful exposure at the printing stage and matching it with a suitable grade of paper.

The grade of paper determines how the range of tones in a negative reproduce in a photograph. For example, a high-contrast or overdeveloped negative is better suited to print on a soft grade of paper, whereas a low contrast or underdeveloped negative needs to be printed on a hard grade of paper.

Papers are obtainable from grade 0 (soft) to grade 5 (hard). The majority of black and white negatives require grades 2 or 3. But instead of keeping boxes of various grades of paper on the darkroom shelf you can use a variable-contrast paper. Any grade can be obtained from one box by using different coloured filters which change the contrast response of the paper. For economy, it is possible to buy a kit of filters designed to go into the enlarger's filter drawer (if it has one) or immediately below the lens.

When making enlargements remember that printing paper with a glossy surface is best when you are supplying photographs for reproduction. Choose resin-coated paper to give you short washing times; it also dries quickly.

When producing black and white enlargements the correct exposure can be achieved by making a test strip. After you have decided on the size of the enlargement, and the image on the masking frame is in sharp focus at the widest aperture, stop down the lens by two or three stops and switch off the lamp. Cut a strip from a sheet from the packet of paper you intend to use to make an enlargement. Position the unexposed strip on the masking frame over the most important part of the image.

With a sheet of opaque card which is larger than the test strip, shield the paper before switching on the enlarger lamp. Expose the paper by progressively moving the card in a series of steps and uncovering the paper every five seconds. This will give a test strip of five, ten, fifteen and twenty seconds. Ensure that the strip receives full development.

If there is an indication that it is too dark, repeat the process with reduced exposure or close the lens aperture by an additional stop. If all the steps are too light, increase the exposure accordingly. Never decide which is the correct exposure by safelight illumination. After fixing the paper, switch on the main light for an accurate appraisal.

When handling light-sensitive materials such as printing paper, get into the habit of closing a box or packet immediately after you have removed a sheet from the pack. If you are exposing a number of sheets before developing them, keep them in a separate light-tight box specifically designated for the purpose. By observing a safety system, you will minimize the chances of fogging a lot of unexposed sheets of printing paper when you switch on the main light to examine prints after fixing them.

Creative Techniques

One of the benefits of printing from black and white negatives is the freedom you have to transform the image creatively. Merely by giving more or less exposure to selected areas of a print at the enlarging stage you can improve an excessively light or dark area and increase the overall impact of the picture. Specific techniques in varying the exposure are known as shading, dodging and burning-in.

For large areas which require less exposure, shading can be done by using your hand or holding a piece of card between the lens and paper on the enlarger baseboard during the main exposure. Holding the card between the lens and the baseboard but in the beam of the enlarger lamp will create a shadow over the area which requires less exposure. Aim to keep the shadow moving slightly so that the variation in exposure does not cause hard edges.

Dodging is similar to shading but is used for holding back light from small areas. Make a dodging tool by cutting a small piece of opaque card to the shape of the area to receive less exposure, but smaller. The card should be taped on to the end of a piece of rigid wire. Remember to keep the card moving during exposure to prevent dark edges appearing on the print. The thin wire handle should not affect the exposure of the print.

Burning-in is a technique applied after the main exposure. It involves using a piece of card with a hole cut out of the middle so that extra exposure can be given to an area that requires to be made darker without affecting the remainder of the print. Again, endeavour to keep the card moving throughout the additional exposure and hold the card well above the printing paper on the baseboard.

Dodging or burning-in can transform an ordinary image into a striking photograph. As you become more familiar with darkroom procedure you will be more adept in using these skills. Do not be discouraged by the inevitable spoiled prints. Analyse the disappointing results and consider them as part of the learning process. Enrolling for a photography evening class or joining a camera club can be beneficial for anyone contemplating developing and printing. The best way of learning darkroom techniques is to watch someone practising them.

Whether you are looking through the viewfinder of your camera or producing prints in the darkroom, it is advisable to follow a set routine. You can then more easily determine what you need to improve and gain the maximum benefit from your photography. As you become more skilful and successful, capturing pictures for publication will be a stimulating extension of your writing.

Photographic Glossary

Aperture Within the lens, a circular opening through which light passes. In all but very simple cameras it can be adjusted, controlling the volume of light from the subject to the film.

Aperture-priority AE An automatic exposure mode in which the photographer chooses the aperture and the camera sets the appropriate shutter speed.

APS Advanced Photo System.

Auto-exposure A system in which a photosensitive cell measures the available light and sets the appropriate aperture, shutter speed, or both.

Auto-flash A self-activating facility in low light.

Auto-focus An electronic system which focuses automatically on the subject without any manual adjustment.

Bracketing A method used in situations when correct exposure is difficult to achieve. Additional shots are taken at one aperture stop or half stop above and below the indicated exposure.

B-setting Used for long exposures. The shutter remains open for as long as the release is depressed.

Cable release An attachment which enables the shutter to be fired without touching the camera. Useful for long exposures when the camera is mounted on a tripod.

CCD A charge-coupled device chip of picture elements (pixels). When an exposure is made on a digital camera and light reaches a CCD it creates an electrical charge which is converted into a digital image.

CD-writer A device that enables you to store digital photographs on writable CDs.

Dedicated flashgun A flashgun designed to be used on a particular camera or brand of camera.

Depth of field The area in front of and behind the point of focus in which the subject is acceptably sharp.

Depth of field preview A camera control which enables you to view the image through the selected aperture to check how much of the scene is sharp.

DX-coding A code on a film cassette which is read by the camera and automatically sets the correct ISO film speed.

F-stop The size of the aperture through which light passes to the film. The lower the number, the larger the aperture, the higher the number, the smaller the aperture.

Fill-in flash mode When the central subject is darker than the backlighting, a means of providing the exact amount of flash to balance the subject with the backlighting.

Film speed An indication of a film's sensitivity to light expressed as an ISO number. The higher the number the more sensitive the film is to light.

Focal length With the lens focused on infinity, the distance from the optical centre of the lens to the focal plane of the film.

Focus lock If the shutter release button is partially pressed, it allows you to focus on an off-centre subject and compose the picture in the viewfinder while maintaining the subject in focus.

Hot shoe A fitting on a camera that allows a flashgun to be attached to the top-plate, to be directly connected electrically, and to be fired in synchronization with the shutter.

ISO International Standards Organisation. The ISO number denotes the film speed.

LCD Liquid crystal display. Computer-style information displayed on or in a camera. On digital cameras it refers to the flat viewing screen which enables you to see the pictures you have taken.

LED Light-emitting diode. Provides information in the viewfinder or on the top-plate.

Lens hood An attachment which prevents unwanted light reaching the lens.

Macro-lens A lens with a focusing range from infinity to very close range (usually down to 1:2 or 1:1) without the use of additional attachments.

Megapixels Digital cameras with a resolution of over one million pixels.

Memory cards Cards which store images from a digital camera until they are transferred to a computer. They can then be wiped clean and reused.

Pixel A picture element. The larger the number of pixels a digital camera has, the finer the quality of the digital image.

Photo CD A CD which stores pictures and also enables you to enhance scanned images on a computer.

Program AE An automatic exposure mode which sets the aperture and shutter speed.

Red-eye reduction A flash mode which fires pre-flashes to minimize the problem of red-eye in pictures.

Self-timer A device for delaying the release of the shutter, typically for ten seconds although some have a variety of delay periods. Used when the photographer wants to be included in the picture.

Shutter-priority AE An automatic exposure mode which allows you to set the shutter speed, with the camera selecting the appropriate aperture.

Telephoto lens A long-focal length lens; magnification is greater than with the standard lens, and distant subjects are brought closer.

Wide-angle lens A lens with a short focal length which has an angle of view that is wider than the human eye.

Zoom lens A lens which can be adjusted to cover a range of variable focal lengths.

Index